BILBO'S
JOURNEY

BÏLBO'S JOURNEY

Discovering the Hidden Meaning of *The Hobbit*

Joseph Pearce

SAINT BENEDICT+PRESS
Charlotte, North Carolina

Cover design by Milo Persic.

Cover image by Lourdes Velez Campos.
www.belegilgalad.deviantart.com

Cataloging-in-Publication data on file with the Library of Congress.
Pearce, Joseph, 1961-
    Bilbo's journey : discovering the hidden meaning of The hobbit / Joseph Pearce.
        p. cm.
        Includes bibliographical references.
        ISBN 978-1-61890-058-6
1. Tolkien, J. R. R. (John Ronald Reuel), 1892-1973. Hobbit. 2. Fantasy fiction, English—History and criticism. I. Title.
PR6039.O32H6356 2012
823'.912--dc23   2012037491

Published in the United States by Saint Benedict Press, LLC
PO Box 410487
Charlotte, NC 28241
www.saintbenedictpress.com

Printed and bound in the United States of America.

For Jef and Lorraine Murray
and all who are hobbits at heart

TABLE OF CONTENTS

CHAPTER 1

BILBO'S PILGRIMAGE

J. R. R. TOLKIEN'S first work of fiction, *The Hobbit*, is often overlooked in favor of its epic follow-up, *The Lord of the Rings*. And not without reason. *The Lord of the Rings* carries a depth of meaning and an overall quality that outstrips its predecessor. It is also a publishing phenomenon. Since its initial publication, almost sixty years ago, more than 150 million copies of *The Lord of the Rings* have been sold. Furthermore, Tolkien's epic has triumphed over all its literary rivals in numerous opinion polls. A survey organized jointly by a major bookselling chain and a national TV network in the UK in 1996 revealed that *The Lord of the Rings* topped the poll in 104 of the 105 branches of the bookstore, receiving 20 percent more votes than its nearest rival, George Orwell's *Nineteen Eighty-four*. It triumphed in similar fashion in other surveys conducted by the BBC, by national newspapers, and by literary societies. Perhaps its ultimate triumph in the age of the internet was its being voted best book of the millennium by

Amazon.com customers, signaling its conquest of the final frontier of cyberspace.

Not surprisingly, in the wake of the book's phenomenal success, Peter Jackson's three-part movie adaptation of *The Lord of the Rings* became one of the most successful films of all time. In December 2012, a decade after *The Lord of the Rings* was premiered, the first part of Jackson's three-part adaptation of *The Hobbit* was released in movie theaters around the world. As the movie takes the world by storm, Bilbo Baggins is set to take the limelight from Frodo, his more famous and illustrious nephew. These are indeed heady days for the relatively simple children's story, originally published in 1937, which would pave the way for its author's far more ambitious epic, published almost twenty years later.

It should come as no surprise that Jackson's movie is not strictly speaking a children's film. The producer forged his reputation as a maker of gruesome horror movies and does not do Disney schmaltz (Deo gratias!). Containing a degree of violence and an array of monsters, including giant spiders, trolls, orcs, a fearsome dragon, and the incomparably creepy Gollum, the film is not for the very young or the timid. Younger children, who might have enjoyed the book, will find the violence a little unsettling and the visualization of the monstrous the very stuff of which nightmares are made.

On the other hand, it should be stressed that *The Hobbit* is much more than a simple children's story and that any dumbing down of the gravitas of its moral dimension would do much more damage to the integrity of the work than the graphic depiction of violence and the frightening presentation of the monstrous. At its deepest level of meaning—and great children's literature always has a deep level of meaning—*The Hobbit* is a pilgrimage of grace, in which its protagonist, Bilbo Baggins, becomes grown-up in the most important sense, which is the growth in wisdom and virtue. Throughout the course of his adventure—and every pilgrimage is an adventure—the hobbit develops the habit of virtue and grows in sanctity. Thus *The Hobbit* illustrates the priceless truth that we only become wise men (homo sapiens) when we realize that we are pilgrims on a purposeful journey through life (homo viator).

Apart from the story's status as a Christian *bildungsroman*, charting Bilbo's rite of passage from ignorance to wisdom and from bourgeois vice to heroic virtue, *The Hobbit* parallels *The Lord of the Rings* in the mystical suggestiveness of its treatment of Divine Providence, and serves as a moral commentary on the words of Christ that "where your treasure is, there your heart will be also" (Matthew 6:21). In these three aspects, it can truly be said of *The Hobbit*, as Tolkien said of *The Lord of the Rings*, that it is "a fundamentally religious and Catholic work."[1]

On one level, Bilbo's journey from the homely comfort of the Shire to the uncomfortable lessons learned on the Lonely Mountain, in parallel with Frodo's journey from the Shire to Mount Doom, is a mirror of Everyman's journey through life. It is in this sense that Tolkien wrote in his celebrated and cerebral essay "On Fairy Stories" that "the fairy-story . . . may be used as a *Mirour de l'Omme*" or as "the Mirror of scorn and pity towards Man."[2] In short, we are meant to see ourselves reflected in the character of Bilbo Baggins and our lives reflected in his journey from the Shire to the Lonely Mountain. How is this? Clearly, we are not hobbits, literally speaking, nor could we ever journey with dwarves through the Misty Mountains and Mirkwood, encountering goblins and elves en route, except vicariously by allowing our imagination, as readers, to follow in Bilbo's footsteps. In order to see the story as Tolkien wishes us to see it, we have to transcend the literal meaning of the story and ascend to the level of moral and anagogical applicability.

For the Christian, who spurns the nihilism of the existentialist, life is charged with meaning and purpose and is at the service of the final goal and purpose of every human life, which is its being united with the Divine Life of God in heaven. This being so, every life should be a quest to achieve the goal of heaven through a growth in virtue, thereby attaining the power, through grace, to overcome the monsters and demons which seek to prevent the achievement of this paramount goal. It is in this way and with this understanding of the meaning and purpose of life that we are meant to read *The Hobbit* and it is in this way, and this way alone, that we find its deepest and most applicable meaning.

Another key component of *The Hobbit*, which it shares with *The Lord of the Rings*, is the presence of the invisible hand of Providence or grace. This invisible hand, euphemistically labeled "luck" in the story, has led to a degree of misunderstanding on the part of many critics. Colin Manlove is typical of those who see the presence of such "luck" as a literary weakness, describing it as "the continued presence of biased fortune." Manlove complains that "a whole skein of apparent coincidences" signifies that "[i]t is not moral will but luck which is the architect of success." In the presence of such "biased fortune" or "luck," Manlove argues that the struggle with evil in Tolkien's work is "mere posturing in a rigged boat."[3] Such criticism lacks subtlety because it fails to see the subtlety at work in the narrative. As Gandalf makes plain at the book's conclusion, what had been called "luck" was not really "luck" at all. "You don't really suppose, do you," Gandalf tells Bilbo, "that all your adventures and escapes were managed by mere luck . . . ?"

Pace Manlove, "moral will" is never sufficient in itself as "the architect of success," either in Middle-earth or in the wider world in which we live. Contrary to the claims of Nietzsche, Hitler, and other secular "progressives," there is no triumph of the will without the supernatural assistance of grace. This is the whole point of Frodo's failure to destroy the Ring of his own volition in *The Lord of the Rings*. "Moral will," on its own, is never enough. An outside agent, i.e. grace, is always necessary. Thus it is Gollum, ironically and paradoxically, who is the unwitting agent of grace at the climactic moment on Mount Doom. Yet his sudden appearance at the crucial moment is not mere "luck," if by "luck" we mean mere chance. He is there because his life had been spared at earlier crucial moments by Bilbo, Frodo, and Sam, all of whom, at various times, had been tempted to kill their enemy when the opportunity presented itself. In each case, the hobbits chose mercy and pity over the desire for vengeance. These successive acts of virtue, of loving their enemy instead of hating him, were moral tests, the passing of which was necessary to the defeat of evil. Having passed the test, Gollum's appearance at the crucial moment was the hobbits' reward for the passing of the test, an unexpected but necessary gift, given to them by the same invisible Hand which had given them the earlier tests. This is not "luck" but providence.

In *The Hobbit*, as in *The Lord of the Rings*, good "luck" is inextricably connected to good choices and bad "luck" is inextricably connected to bad choices. With regard to the latter, we should recall the words of Gandalf to Pippin that "[o]ften does hatred hurt itself"[4] or the words of Theoden that "oft evil will shall evil mar."[5] Thus, there is a supernatural dimension to the unfolding of events in Middle-earth, in which Tolkien shows the mystical balance that exists between the promptings of grace, or of demonic temptation, and the response of the will to such promptings and temptations. This mystical relationship plays itself out in the form of transcendent providence, which is much more than "luck" or chance. For a Christian, this is life as it is. It is realism. A Christian believes in dragons, even if he can't see them, and knows that they are perilous and potentially deadly. They are certainly not to be courted, nor is it wise to toy with them. "The more truly we can see life as a fairytale," said the great G. K. Chesterton, "the more clearly the tale resolves itself into war with the dragon who is wasting fairyland."[6]

Returning to Manlove's misapprehension about the nature of "luck" in Middle-earth, or "biased fortune" as he calls it, we can see his error in describing the struggle with evil in Tolkien's work as "mere posturing in a rigged boat." The truth is that "fortune" in Middle-earth, and in the world beyond it, is biased in both directions. On the one hand, grace is always available to those who seek it and ask for it, biasing "fortune" in the direction of goodness; yet, on the other hand, the fallenness of nature means that man's natural tendency is towards concupiscence and its destructive consequences. If we don't ask for help, we are bound to fall. It is in this choice, rooted in the gift and responsibility of free will, that the struggle with evil is won or lost. The will must willingly cooperate with grace or, in its failure to do so, must inevitably fall into evil. Far from the struggle being a "mere posturing in a rigged boat," it is a dangerous adventure in a perilous realm.

If the interplay of providence and free will is the means by which the dynamism of virtue and its consequences drive the narrative forward, the overarching moral of *The Hobbit* would appear to be a cautionary meditation on Matthew 6:21 (*where your treasure is, there your heart will be also*).

The Hobbit begins with Bilbo's desire for comfort and his unwillingness to sacrifice himself for others. His heart is essentially self-centered, surrounding itself with the treasures of his own home, an ironic and symbolic prefiguring of Smaug's surrounding himself with treasure in his "home" in the Lonely Mountain. Bilbo, on a microcosmic scale, is, therefore, nothing less than a figure and prefigurement of Smaug the dragon. He is afflicted with the dragon sickness. His pilgrimage to the Lonely Mountain is the means by which he will be cured of this materialist malady. It is a via dolorosa, a path of suffering, the following of which will heal him of his self-centeredness and teach him to give himself self-sacrificially to others.

The paradoxical consequence of the dragon sickness is that the things possessed possess the possessor, much as the possession of the Ring in the later book leads to those who wear it becoming possessed by their possession. In the case of the Ring, the bearer of it can resist its power only by refusing to succumb to the temptation to wield its power by wearing it. In other words, the Ring's malevolent power over the one who carries it is directly connected to the degree of attachment that the bearer has towards it. The more detached the bearer is from his possession, the less possessed is he by it. In similar fashion Bilbo is far too attached to his own possessions at the beginning of the story, not for their own sakes but for the pleasure that they offer. His possessions are not valued for the power that they wield, as is the case with the Ring, but for their ability to supply a soporific comfort. Although he only values his possessions as a means to an end, and not as an end in themselves, the fact that they are necessary, or so he thinks, to the attainment of the creature comforts that he craves, bestows upon them a power over their possessor which is akin to possession of him. Thus Bilbo is a slave to his possessions at the beginning of the story and is liberated from them, or from his addiction to them, by its end. Similarly Smaug is a prisoner of his own treasure-hoard, unable to leave his brooding over his possessions for fear that someone might steal something. The dragon's sickness is especially ironic because it is clear that Smaug has no practical use for any of the treasure. He is a slave of something that is essentially useless to him. His dragon-heart is possessed by the addiction to something which, for a dragon, is nothing but trivia and trash.

Ultimately, as we shall see as we follow Bilbo on his pilgrimage from the Shire to the Lonely Mountain and back again, *The Hobbit* is not merely about slaying the dragon who is wasting fairy land but is also, and more importantly, about slaying the dragon who is attempting to waste our own souls. Even as Bilbo wanders further from his own home, the truth that he exemplifies is always close to home for each of us as readers. Each of us is prone to the ill effects of the dragon sickness and each of us needs to walk with Bilbo so that we may be healed from its potentially deadly consequences. With this sobering and sanctifying thought in mind, let's make the pilgrimage with Bilbo, following in his furry footsteps on the path of grace.

CHAPTER 2

An Unexpected Parting

In a hole in the ground there lived a hobbit. Not a nasty, dirty, wet hole, filled with the ends of worms and an oozy smell, nor yet a dry, bare, sandy hole with nothing in it to sit down on or to eat: it was a hobbit-hole, and that means comfort.[1]

T HE OPENING sentence of *The Hobbit* is one of the most famous first sentences in all of literature. Simple and short, like its subject, it ignites the imagination the moment we read it. What on earth, and in its comfortable hole in the earth, is a hobbit? Unlike orcs, elves, dwarves, wizards, and trolls, all of which Tolkien had trawled from the deep cauldron of myth, which is the common inheritance of the civilized imagination, hobbits were apparently entirely new, springing forth as an imaginative fruit from the fertile soul of the author. And yet, as Tolkien would be the first to insist, it is not strictly accurate or adequate to describe anything, even hobbits, as *entirely* new. Although hobbits were making their literary debut in Tolkien's book, they could not be *entirely* new because nothing under the sun is entirely new. It is for this reason that Tolkien made the important and necessary distinction between Creation and sub-creation. Only God creates, in the sense of making something out of nothing (*ex nihilo*), whereas artists and authors merely sub-create, making things from other things that already exist. Thus Tolkien's newly sub-created hobbits were themselves composed of ingredients that Tolkien borrowed from other sources. Even the very word "hobbit" does not originate with Tolkien, even though he is normally attributed with coining it. "Hobbits" appear in an obscure list of supernatural creatures composed by the nineteenth century folklorist, Michael Aislabie Denham. Curiously, the word is not found anywhere else, suggesting that it was a colloquialism for a ghost of some sort which Denham had come across in his study of the oral folkloric traditions of northern England and Scotland. Although we don't know whether Tolkien ever read the little-known book, published by the Folklore Society in 1895,[2] in which the word made its only known appearance in print, it would not be too surprising if he had. Few people were more widely read in folklore than Tolkien. Had he been struck by the word when first reading it in the midst of Denham's long list of ghostly creatures? Did he resurrect it, consciously or unconsciously, when he wrote the first line of his own book?

Regardless of whether Tolkien may have borrowed the word from the earlier obscure source, his hobbits have nothing in common with Denham's. They are not ghoulish ghosts, by any stretch of the imagination. When one thinks of Tolkien's hobbits, one thinks of the juxtaposition of "home" and "habit" or even "rabbit" (considering their burrowed homes and their large furry feet). We feel very much at home in their presence because the hobbits are very close to home. In truth, Bilbo Baggins bears a remarkable resemblance to each of us, his diminutive size and furry feet notwithstanding. He is a gentleman, much like Tolkien and his readers, who seeks the respectable life of bourgeois gentility. Indeed, we are told on the very first page that Bilbo "was a very well-to-do hobbit" and that he came from a very respectable family: "people considered [the Bagginses] very respectable, not only because most of them were rich, but also because they never had any adventures or did anything unexpected."[3] Bilbo likes tea and toast, and jam and pickles; he has wardrobes full of clothes and lots of pantries full of food; he likes the view from his own window and has no desire to see the view from distant windows, let alone the view from distant mountains and valleys. He is a creature of comfort dedicated to the creature comforts. Nothing could be further from Bilbo Baggins' mind, or further from his desire, than the prospect, or the threat, of an adventure. In Christian terms, Bilbo Baggins is dedicated to the easy life and would find the prospect of taking up his cross and following the heroic path of self-sacrifice utterly anathema. The unexpected party at the beginning of the story, in which the daily habits of the hobbit are disrupted by the arrival of unwelcome guests is, therefore, a necessary disruption. It is the intervention into his cozy life of an element of inconvenience or suffering which serves as a wake-up call and a call to action. Gandalf introduces the reluctant Bilbo to Thorin Oakenshield and the other dwarves in order to prompt him into an adventure, the purpose of which is ostensibly the recovery of the dwarves' treasure but also, on the moral level at which the story works, the growth in wisdom and virtue, through suffering and sacrifice, of Bilbo himself. In losing his bourgeois respectability, the price he must pay for becoming an adventurer and "burglar," he forsakes the world and the worldly in favor of the pearl of great price.

The fact that Bilbo is comfortably or uncomfortably like his readers is accentuated in the opening pages of the book by the narrator's revelation that hobbits have "little or no magic about them, except the ordinary everyday sort which helps them to disappear quietly and quickly when large stupid folk like you and me come blundering along, making a noise like elephants which they can hear a mile off."[4] Hobbits are, therefore, not magical at all, except to the degree that they are closely connected to their natural surroundings and can detect through their finely tuned senses the arrival of heavy-footed and heavy-handed strangers. They could, in fact, be said to be more *natural* than "folk like you and me." What might appear magical to us, in our modern artificial and urbanized understanding of things, is merely the most natural thing in the world. The hobbits' power to "disappear" before we see them is the same power that deer and other wild animals possess. It is also, no doubt, the same power that our own ancestors possessed before modernity desensitized us to our natural surroundings. Ironically, therefore, the hobbits are more natural than we are. They are also, shock of shocks, less "magical" than we are, a fact that will not be grasped until we understand Tolkien's understanding of magic and his treatment of it in his work.

Broadly speaking, the things that are considered "magic" in Middle-earth fall into three categories: the natural, the technological, and the supernatural. The first kind of "magic" is the "ordinary everyday sort" which hobbits possess in common with wild animals and our own ancestors. This is purely natural and only appears to be magic to those who have lost touch with the dignity of nature and their place within it. The second kind of "magic" is the use of technology to do things that are not possible without it. In historical terms, this sort of magic was the preserve of the alchemists, the progenitors of modern science, who conducted experiments in a quest to domineer nature. Thus the early alchemists sought the philosopher's stone in order to turn base metal into gold and the elixir of life to defeat death and attain immortality. The philosopher's stone was desired so that men might become rich beyond their wildest dreams. Thus, in the language of *The Hobbit*, the early alchemists were suffering from the dragon sickness. Their magic was scientific and yet unwholesome and unhealthy. Although the alchemists have yet to discover the philosopher's stone and the elixir of life, their desire for wealth and their urge to defeat death and aging are still the primary motives for those modern alchemists who employ scientific research for the purposes of wealth and power. It must be conceded, however, that scientific research has brought forth many technological fruits which most of us would consider indispensable. Furthermore, man has learned to do things that our ancestors would certainly have considered magical. We can fly, not merely in the sky above our heads but to the very moon! We can make huge cities disappear with the magical splitting of tiny atoms. This is clever. It is magical. But is it wise? Is it good?

For Tolkien, most of the fruits of modern technology have proved harmful to humanity and harmful to the harmony of the natural ordering of things. He would rather live naturally with hobbits in the Shire than unnaturally with his contemporaries in the noisy business of modern cities. Indeed, as he readily admitted, his creation of the Shire was a means of escaping the nastiness of the modern city. We might not fully agree with Tolkien but insofar as we enjoy escaping with him to Middle-earth we are at least sympathizing with his predilections.

Considering Tolkien's distaste for technological magic we should not be surprised to discover that this sort of magic is the preserve of the evil characters in Middle-earth. In *The Lord of the Rings*, Sauron and Saruman lay waste to the beauty of the natural world in order to fuel their prideful desire to dominate nature and destroy its natural goodness.

The third kind of "magic" in Middle-earth is supernatural magic, or what more correctly, at least in its positive manifestations, should be called "miracle." Gandalf's "magic" in *The Lord of the Rings* is of this sort, most obviously in his revelation of himself on the Bridge of Khazad-dûm as "a servant of the Secret Fire" who has power over "the Shadow" and its "dark fire" and also in his transfiguration and resurrection in Fangorn Forest. By comparison,

Gandalf's power in *The Hobbit* often resembles the mere trickery of the common or garden wizard of popular fiction, indicative of the earlier work's relative shallowness in this respect. The other manifestation of supernatural "magic" in Middle-earth is the demonic power wielded by Sauron, which is present potently in *The Lord of the Rings* but largely absent from *The Hobbit*.

This tangential aside on the nature and supernature of the various kinds of "magic" in Middle-earth is not only necessary for the clarity of our understanding of Tolkien's oeuvre but also as a means of detecting a very real difference between *The Hobbit* and the later work of which it is the precursor. With the exception of the power wielded by Gandalf, *The Hobbit* is noteworthy in relation to *The Lord of the Rings* for the relative absence of magic, notwithstanding the "magical" power it wields over us as readers.

Gandalf's unexpected arrival at Bilbo's home at the beginning of the story startles us with the way that he brings dead words to life. Bilbo had greeted him by saying "good morning," a phrase that is all too often employed unthinkingly. There can, however, be no such subconscious or somnambulant speech in Gandalf's presence. He insists that we are alive to the rich meaning of the words we use. "What do you mean?" he asks. "Do you wish me a good morning, or mean that it is a good morning whether I want it or not; or that you feel good this morning; or that it is a morning to be good on?"[5] In Gandalf's opening words, therefore, the words that Bilbo uses are made flesh. They are given substance, or meaning. One might even say that

a form of transubstantiation has taken place. The outward appearance or sound of the words remains the same, their accidental qualities, but they are enfleshed with meaning, and not only meaning but multiple meanings, signifying that one solitary phrase can feed a multitude of thoughts. For Gandalf, words are the gateway to reality, the means by which we engage with the objective truth beyond ourselves. He is the opposite of the postmodernist who argues that because a single word can be the key to the opening of numerous meanings, there is no such thing as objective meaning. Gandalf represents the antithesis of such nonsense and the antidote to its poison.

The wizard's unexpected arrival is connected to his desire to wake Bilbo up from his cozy slumbers. In doing so, he also wakes us up from ours. It is for this reason that he wishes to send Bilbo on an adventure, which, he informs the hobbit, will be "very good for you—and profitable too, very likely, if you ever get over it."[6] Bilbo is not convinced. He has "no use for adventures," which are "uncomfortable things."[7] Little does he know it, but the fact that adventures are uncomfortable is the very reason for their usefulness. Gandalf wants to remove Bilbo from his comfort zone so that the hobbit can experience reality in its full and expansive richness. Bilbo needs to venture beyond his home, which is an extension of his self, in order to experience the truth that is beyond himself and grow in the space that it provides. In short, the purpose of Gandalf's visit is to help Bilbo grow-up.

The beginning of Bilbo's unexpected and unwelcome adventure is the arrival of the unexpected and

unwelcome dwarves, at Gandalf's invitation, on the following day. Much to the hobbit's discomfort, it becomes increasingly clear that, at Gandalf's behest, they intend for Bilbo to
join them in a perilous quest to liberate treasure from the
clutches of a dragon. As Thorin discusses the nature of the
quest, the motif of the dragon sickness is first established.
Dragons steal gold and jewels and guard them possessively
for the rest of their lives, even though they "never enjoy a
brass ring of it." They "hardly know a good bit of work from
a bad, though they usually have a good notion of the current
market value; and they can't make a thing for themselves,
not even mend a little loose scale of their armour."[8] Thorin's
depiction of the dragons of Middle-earth seems uncannily
like the description of certain types of people, which all of
us know; those who, like Oscar Wilde's cynic, know the
price of everything and the value of nothing. From the start,
therefore, the dragons are more than simply dragons; they
are also signifiers of a certain attitude to life and to things,
which is ultimately unhealthy and is rightly considered a
sickness.

Continuing his exposition on the nature of dragons,
Thorin tells Bilbo that dragons also "carry away people,
especially maidens, to eat."[9] Once again, the fullness of
applicable meaning transcends the literal eating of the
flesh of maidens. Dragons are not merely hungry, they are
wicked. They desire the defilement of the pure and unde-
filed, the destruction of the virgin. Their devouring is a
deflowering. Parallels with human "dragons" in the world
beyond Middle-earth and closer to the home of the reader
are not difficult to discern. The war against the dragon is

not, therefore, a war against a physical monster, like a dinosaur, but a battle against the wickedness we encounter in our everyday lives. We all face our daily dragons and we must all defend ourselves from them and hopefully slay them. The sobering reality is that we must either fight the dragons that we encounter in life or become dragons ourselves. There is no "comfortable" alternative. This is the reason that the unexpected party at the beginning of *The Hobbit* becomes the unexpected parting of Bilbo from all the comforts of home. He sets out as the most reluctant pilgrim and adventurer that can be imagined, bemoaning his "luck" and resenting Gandalf's disruption of his somnambulant existence. It would take many days and a great deal of discomfort before Bilbo would come to realize the truth of Gandalf's words that the adventure would be very good for him—and profitable.

CHAPTER 3

TRUSTING IN "LUCK"

THE FIRST peril that Bilbo and the dwarves face after setting off from the Shire is a deadly encounter with three man-eating (and hobbit-eating and dwarf-eating) trolls. Although Bilbo manages to scurry to safety, observing events while hiding in a thorn-bush, the dwarves are all captured and seem destined to serve as a veritable feast of a supper. All seems lost until a mysterious voice, soon revealed to be as belonging to Gandalf, mimicking each of the trolls in turn, foments discord amongst them. Each believing that the voice belongs to one of the others, the trolls continue to argue about the best way to cook or kill the dwarves until the first light of the sun appears above the horizon, at which point all three are turned to stone, as is the fate of trolls who do not return to the shadows beneath the mountain before daylight.

In spite of the perilous scenario, the whole episode descends dangerously close to the level of bathos. The incongruous juxtaposition of the deadly situation and the clownish cockney dialogue of the trolls themselves, accentuated by their cockney names of Bill, Bert, and Tom, seems to militate against the decorum and gravitas of the predicament in which the dwarves find themselves. Bill is even given the decidedly cockney-sounding surname of "Huggins" reminding this reader at least of Henry Higgins (or 'Enry 'Iggins) in George Bernard Shaw's *Pygmalion*. Although Tolkien would retain cockney as the dialect of the orcs in *The Lord of the Rings*, the employment of the vulgar vernacular is handled with a subtlety and dexterity in the later work which is largely absent in *The Hobbit*, nor does Tolkien make the disastrous and egregious error in the later work of giving cockney-sounding names to the Uruk-hai!

The comic element to this scene might be heightened by Gandalf's mimicry but it should not be allowed to obscure the more serious dimension of the wizard's ploy to delay the trolls until sunrise. In an echo of the wisdom of his words in *The Lord of the Rings* that "[o]ften does hatred hurt itself," Gandalf uses the natural negativity of the trolls to destroy them. As creatures of darkness, they lack charity and are prone to quarrel, much as we see the orcs doing often in *The Lord of the Rings*, and Gandalf, employing what might be called a form of spiritual jujitsu, uses the weight of the trolls' own sinfulness to bring about their own downfall. Fallen already into sin, they are all too ready to fall into the folly that will be their undoing.

Gandalf's scheme of delaying the devilish devices of the trolls until their undoing at dawn is reminiscent of Hilaire Belloc's telling of the tale of St. Dunstan in *The Four Men* and it is tempting to see Belloc's earlier work as an influence on this episode in *The Hobbit*. Belloc recounts the legend that St. Dunstan, the tenth century monk and Archbishop of Canterbury, had dared the devil to destroy the county of Sussex by digging a hole through the South Downs, thereby causing the sea to submerge the flat land of the Sussex Weald which lay beyond the hills. The devil had claimed in his pride that he could dig through the Downs in a solitary night and St. Dunstan therefore extracted from him the promise that the devil would leave Sussex in peace if he failed: "if you have not done it by the time the cock crows over the Weald, you shall depart in God's name."[1] It looked as though the devil might win the wager as he dug a huge gorge in the Downs, which today is known as Devil's Dyke, but St. Dunstan outwitted the devil by praying that all the cocks of Sussex might crow earlier than usual, fooling Satan into believing that dawn had arrived and that, therefore, he had lost the bet. By the time that the devil realized the trick that had been played on him it was too late. He had lost the precious time he needed to complete his evil task and, as the dawn broke in the east, "with a great howl the Devil was aware that his wager was lost."[2]

The parallels between the two stories, in which devilish work is delayed by virtuous trickery until the dawn brings salvation, are discernible enough. Furthermore, it is very probable that Tolkien knew Belloc's *Four Men* very well. Belloc and his friend Chesterton were almost obligatory reading for young and literary-minded Catholics of Tolkien's generation and the period of Tolkien's formative reading coincided exactly with the Edwardian period during which Belloc and Chesterton were at their most popular.[3] The influence of Chesterton on Tolkien is well-documented and is evident in Tolkien's positive appraisal of Chesterton's work in his essay "On Fairy Stories." Although Belloc's influence is less obvious, Tolkien's description of the blizzard on Caradhras in *The Lord of the Rings* resonates strikingly with Belloc's description of a blizzard on the Alps in *The Path to Rome*, and Tolkien's respect for Belloc was evident in a conversation with the Jesuit priest, Martin D'Arcy, notwithstanding Tolkien's lack of sympathy with Belloc's Francophilia and Germanophobia.[4]

If the perilous encounter with the trolls is spoiled somewhat by the bathetic way in which it is told, at least for those readers who prefer the mythic gravitas of *The Lord of the Rings* to the relative flippancy of *The Hobbit*, Bilbo's first encounter with the elves is similarly spoiled and anti-climactic. They are heralded by "a burst of song like laughter in the trees,"[5] which conveys something of the mystique of Faerie that Tolkien achieves in the later book and in works such as *Smith of Wootton Major*, but the effect is lost instantly by the bathetic descent into the "tra-la-la-lally" of the trite and trivial ditty that follows. There are hints of the elvish powers which are so impressive in *The Lord of the Rings*, such as the narrator's parenthetical aside that it is foolish to think that elves are foolish, yet even this cautionary corrective is only necessary because of the rather foolish way in which the narrator had presented them up to this point. How different is Bilbo's first encounter with the frolicking and frivolous elves of *The Hobbit* from Frodo's first encounter with the High Elves in *The Lord of the Rings*, who are heralded by a hymn to Elbereth, as poignant with pathos as the above ditty is burdened with bathos, and which conveys to Catholic ears the beauty and exiled longing of the *Salve Regina*. The difference and dissonance between the two accounts are shocking to such a degree that it could be said that the arrival of the elves in *The Hobbit* does violence to our critical sensibilities in so far as it violates the dignity and solemnity with which the elves are treated in the later work. Such a contrast serves as a timely reminder that it is best to read the books in the order in which they were written. Ideally one should read *The Hobbit* first, enjoying its charm and the moral fabric with which it is woven, before graduating to the later, greater work. If one follows this approach one grows with the story, ascending to heights that are only hinted at in *The Hobbit*. Reading the books in the reverse order must inevitably result in a sense of deflation and disappointment as our high expectations are dashed on the rocks of the narrator's schoolroom flippancy and whimsy. As such, it is a little unfair to compare the two works and yet, of course, the comparison is unavoidable.

Something of the dignity of the elves is restored once Bilbo, Gandalf *et al* meet Elrond. He identifies the swords that had been found in the trolls' lair by reading the runes on them and is clearly knowledgeable about the ancient history of Middle-earth. Apart from his wealth of knowledge, there is a suggestive hint of the great wisdom which will come to the fore in *The Lord of the Rings*. We are told that he does "not altogether approve of dwarves and their love of gold" but that "he hated dragons and their cruel wickedness." These few words display Elrond's own virtuous disposition but also convey an ominous and prophetic allusion to the dragon sickness to which dwarves as well as dragons are prone. Most important of all to the eventual success of the dwarves' and hobbit's quest is Elrond's reading of the moon-letters on their ancient map. As "luck," i.e. providence, would have it, Elrond happens to be reading the map on a midsummer's eve in a crescent moon, which is the only time that the moon-letters are visible.

Let's look a little closer at the utter improbability of Elrond's reading of the map at the precise time at which the letters would be visible. If he had been shown the map during the day, or on any night of the year except midsummer's eve, the letters would have been invisible, and even if, by chance, he'd happened to pick up the map on midsummer's eve, the letters would still have been invisible unless there was a crescent moon. If by some utterly incredible "luck" he had been reading the map at this precise time, he would still not have seen the moon-letters if midsummer's eve was cloudy and the moon concealed. And, of course, if the party had arrived at Rivendell a day later, or a week earlier, the moment would either have passed or would not yet have arrived. In short, the odds against Elrond studying the map at this precise moment are astronomical (literally as well as figuratively)! Clearly such an unlikely coincidence stretches the bounds of credulity to breaking point and beyond. If we believe that everything in the cosmos is governed by mere chance (not that chance can govern anything but let's not quibble!), the sheer improbability of the scenario beggars belief and reduces the credibility of the narrative to the level of the absurd. The only way that the coincidence makes sense and can be seen as credible is through the acceptance of the existence of the hidden hand of providence. Gandalf, in his words to Frodo in *The Lord of the Rings* about Bilbo's finding of the Ring, accepts the existence of such a hand, and the existence of a Divine Will which governs the hand. Describing Bilbo as "the most unlikely person imaginable" to find the Ring, Gandalf concludes that "there was something else at work, beyond any design of the Ring-maker. I can put it no plainer than by saying that Bilbo was *meant* to find the Ring, and *not* by its maker. In which case you also were *meant* to have it. And that may be an encouraging thought."[6]

For those, such as Tolkien and Gandalf, who believe that things are *meant* to happen there is no problem in believing that Elrond was *meant* to be studying the map at this precise moment. "Luck" is not merely chance but is evidence of meaning and purpose in the cosmos. This is, of course, the view of those who believe in a supernatural ordering of reality but will not be accepted by materialists who believe that chance alone is responsible for the enormity and complexity of the cosmos. There is a delicious irony here which cannot pass uncommented upon. Atheistic readers of *The Hobbit* and *The Lord of the Rings* scoff at the improbability and therefore the implausibility of the "luck" with which certain things happen even though their own materialist philosophy is based upon the belief that everything in reality is the product of astronomical "luck," which is billions of times less likely and plausible than Elrond's reading of the moon-letters or Bilbo's finding of the Ring.

If Elrond had seemingly incredible "luck" reading the ancient map at the exact moment at which its secret letters were legible, the cryptic meaning of the secret words themselves suggests that the dwarves and the hobbit will need even greater and even more incredible "luck" if their quest is to be successful. "Stand by the grey stone when the thrush knocks," the moon-letters direct, "and the setting sun with the last light of Durin's Day will shine upon the key-hole."[7] Thorin explains to the puzzled Elrond that Durin's Day only occurs on "the first day of the last moon of Autumn on the threshold of Winter . . . when the last moon of Autumn and the sun are in the sky together."[8]

Again, let's look a little closer at the astronomical odds against the key-hole ever being discovered. The party will need to arrive at the Lonely Mountain in time for the last moon of Autumn. They will then need to locate "the grey stone" somewhere on the mountainside. Having done this, they will need to be there at sunset and hope that in this particular year the sun and moon will be visible together in the sky, thereby making it a "Durin's Day" on which the key-hole can be illuminated by the last rays of the sun. If, by some astonishing "luck," all of these pieces of the puzzle are in place, it will be to no avail unless, by "chance," a thrush happens to be knocking at the precise moment necessary. The chances of such a scenario coming to pass are beyond the bounds of belief in a world in which everything is mere chance and in which no divine help can be relied upon. In such a world, the dwarves and hobbit would have thrown their arms in the air in abject surrender, despairing of the possibility of achieving their goal. They would return home, disconsolate and disillusioned. This is not, however, the sort of world in which they live.

If the finding of the key-hole will take a miracle, they had better hope for the best, which is to hope for the miracle, and make sure that they arrive at the Lonely Mountain in time for a hoped-for Durin's Day and the hoped-for miracle. It is, therefore, with hope in their faithful hearts that the party leaves Rivendell and heads eastwards to the Misty Mountains.

CHAPTER 4

THE CLEVERNESS OF ORCS

A S BILBO, Gandalf and the dwarves press forward, climbing steadily into the midst of the Misty Mountains, it seems that their luck had finally deserted them when all except Gandalf are captured by a party of orcs, or goblins as they are called in *The Hobbit*. We are told by the narrator that "goblins are cruel, wicked, and bad-hearted" and that they "make no beautiful things, but . . . many clever ones":

> It is not unlikely that they invented some of the machines that have since troubled the world, especially the ingenious devices for killing large numbers of people at once, for wheels and engines and explosions always delighted them, and also not working with their own hands more than they could help; but in those days and those wild parts they had not advanced (as it is called) so far.[1]

There is much of Tolkien's own philosophy embedded in the narrator's evident disdain for the goblins which must be understood if we are to understand his work. For Tolkien, echoing the view of the great Greek philosophers, the good, the true, and the beautiful are inextricably interwoven. In Christian terms their unity and inseparability is itself a reflection of the Trinity, Who is the source of all goodness, truth and beauty. This being so, those who are "cruel, wicked, and bad-hearted" will not make good, true or beautiful things. The fact that goblins make "clever" things indicates that intelligence is not a guarantor of goodness, nor is it necessarily a means of finding the truth. Intelligence can be used in the service of cruelty or wickedness, or in the weaving of lies, or in the service of a host of other sins. In the absence of virtue and wisdom, intelligence becomes a servant of evil. It is poisoned. The fact that goblins don't like working with their hands more than they can help illustrates their preference for technology and its "labour saving devices" over the traditional craftsmanship that takes delight in the work of the hands and its products. Compare the goblins' dislike of craftsmanship and art with the delight that elves, hobbits, and dwarves take in such things. Finally, the sardonic irony of the parenthetical comment on so-called "advanced" societies indicates Tolkien's skepticism about the benefits of technological "progress."

In the light of these philosophical musings it is intriguing that the narrator has the goblins leap out of the world of Middle-earth into the world in which we, his readers, live. Crossing the abyss from story to history, from fiction to fact, the narrator suggests that orcs were probably responsible for inventing the weapons of mass destruction which have "since troubled the world." Considering that Tolkien was a veteran of the First World War and had experienced what he described as the "animal horror" of trench warfare[2] and "the carnage of the Somme,"[3] it is not difficult to imagine that "the ingenious devices for killing large numbers of people at once," invented by modern-day orcs, included tanks, machine guns, airplanes, and poison gas. Within ten years of the publication of *The Hobbit* the modern-day goblins would also invent gas chambers and atom bombs.

Writing in January 1945, during the final months of the Second World War, Tolkien lamented the lack of pity shown to the millions of refugees, pouring west to escape the advance of the Soviet army:

> The appalling destruction and misery of this war mount hourly . . . Yet people gloat to hear of the endless lines, 40 miles long, of miserable refugees, women and children pouring West, dying on the way. There seem no bowels of mercy or compassion, no imagination, left in this dark diabolical hour . . . We were supposed to have reached a stage of civilization in which it might still be necessary to execute a criminal, but not to gloat, or to hang his wife and child by him while the orc-crowd hooted . . . Well the first War of the Machines seems to be drawing to its final inconclusive chapter—leaving, alas, everyone the poorer, many bereaved or maimed and millions dead, and only one thing triumphant: the Machines. As the servants of the Machines are becoming a privileged class, the Machines are going to be enormously more powerful. What's their next move?[4]

Their "next move," a few short months later, was the dropping of atomic bombs on defenseless civilians in Hiroshima and Nagasaki, followed by the lurching of the world into a so-called Cold War, in which the overarching strategy was literally and acronymically MAD (mutual assured destruction). In Tolkien's view, there were no winners in a world in which goblin-invented Machines massacre women and children while crowds of orcs hoot their approval.

Compare the narrator's condemnation of goblins in *The Hobbit* with the relative simplicity and sanity of the hobbits of the Shire. Hobbits, the narrator informs us in the prologue to *The Lord of the Rings*, "love peace and quiet and good tilled earth: a well-ordered and well-farmed countryside was their favourite haunt. They do not and did not understand or like machines more complicated than a forge-bellows, a water-mill, or a hand-loom, though they were skilful with tools."[5] After we have made the comparison between the malicious and destructive "cleverness" of the goblins and the gentle and genteel simplicity of the hobbits, we will perceive that the conflict in *The Hobbit* and *The Lord of the Rings* between those who serve the Shadow and those who walk in the Light, between trolls, goblins, and dragons on the one side, and hobbits, dwarves, and elves on the other, is a battle between two civilizations, the culture of death and the culture of life, which is closer to home than we might at first realize. Yet, whether his readers realize it or not, it is abundantly clear that Tolkien understood that his stories were applicable to the world in which his readers lived. *The Hobbit* and *The Lord of the Rings* were imaginative images of the real world and held up a mirror to their readers allowing them to see their own struggles reflected in the stories.

CHAPTER 5

GOLLUM AND THE RING

A FTER BILBO and the dwarves are liberated from the clutches of the goblins by Gandalf's timely intervention, they flee through the subterranean tunnels, deep beneath the Misty Mountains, pursued by a host of goblins intent on avenging the death of their leader, whom Gandalf had slain. In the panic and confusion, Bilbo falls from the back of the dwarf, Dori, who has been carrying him as they fled. He is knocked unconscious and awakes some time later, in the pitch dark and utterly alone. He feels his way, crawling on the ground, "till suddenly his hand met what felt like a tiny ring of cold metal lying on the floor of the tunnel."[1] It was, as the narrator informs us, "a turning point,"[2] not only in Bilbo's own fortunes but, in the light of the later epic, in the fortunes of the whole of Middle-earth. At the time, of course, Bilbo does not know of the Ring's powers and places it in his pocket almost thoughtlessly. At that moment, alone and in the dark, and lost in an orc-infested labyrinth, he has more important things to worry about. Dejected, he feels for his pipe and is pleased to discover that it is not broken. Then he feels for his pouch of pipe-weed and is doubly pleased to discover that it still has some tobacco in it. Feeling much better, he feels for his matches but can find none, which "shatter[s] his hopes completely."[3] Not for the first or last time, Bilbo's bad luck, as he perceives it at the time, is really good "luck." Later, after he comes to his senses, he realizes how dangerous it would have been to have lit a match in the darkness: "Goodness knows what the striking of matches and the smell of tobacco would have brought on him out of dark holes in that horrible place."[4] It was a lucky stroke not being able to make what would have been a very unlucky strike of the match. Once again, however, there is more to "luck" in Middle-earth than meets the eye. If Bilbo had been *meant* to find the Ring, as Gandalf would later tell Frodo, then it is as likely that he was *meant* not to find a match. Even in the darkest depths of the goblin dominions beneath the mountains, Bilbo was being watched by a benign and invisible Presence and being helped by His invisible and providential hand.

In the utter darkness in which he finds himself, Bilbo stumbles on doggedly and almost hopelessly, going down, down into the lowest depths of the subterranean labyrinth. Suddenly he splashes into icy cold water. He has come to a lake that never saw the light of day, in which there dwelt "old Gollum, a small slimy creature . . . as dark as darkness, except for two big round pale eyes in his thin face."[5] Gollum suggests that they play a game of high-stakes riddling in which Gollum agrees to show the hobbit the way out of the labyrinth if Bilbo wins but that the hobbit will be eaten by

Gollum should Bilbo lose. The contest is, therefore, literally a matter of life and death for the hapless hobbit who has little choice but to comply with Gollum's offer. There appears to be no possibility of his finding his own way out of the tunnels alive and the prospect of increasing hunger and exhaustion followed by a slow death by starvation, alone and in the dark, prompts him to accept the rules of the perilous game.

The riddling episode, in which Bilbo and Gollum engage in a war of wits, with so much at stake, is one of the most memorable, exciting, and gripping parts of *The Hobbit*. It draws heavily on Tolkien's knowledge and love of Old English riddles, in which Tolkien shows how much more at home he is with his Christian Saxon ancestors than with his own largely faithless generation. Riddling was a popular pastime amongst the Anglo-Saxons, especially in the monasteries, and there are extant collections of riddles, composed in Latin, by three Catholic saints, St. Aldhelm, Bishop of Sherborne, St. Tatwin, Archbishop of Canterbury, and St. Hwaetberht, Abbot of Wearmouth, a friend of St. Bede. There is also a collection of ninety-five riddles in the Exeter Book, written in Old English, which were well-known to Tolkien.

After the exchange of several riddles, Gollum asks a riddle that seems to have Bilbo beaten:

Alive without breath,
As cold as death:
Never thirsty, ever drinking,
All in mail never clinking.

Desperately trying to think of the correct answer, Bilbo pleads for more time, reminding Gollum that he had given Gollum "a good long chance" when the creature had struggled with the answer of the previous riddle. Gollum, however, is not interested in extending the charity to Bilbo that the hobbit had just extended to him, such a *quid pro quo* not being part of the agreed-upon rules, and demands that Bilbo "must make haste, haste!" As if to emphasize the need for haste, Gollum begins to climb from his boat to get at Bilbo and claim his edible "prize." As he places his foot in the water, a frightened fish jumps from the lake and lands on Bilbo's toes. The hobbit takes the providential hint and shouts out the answer with great relief: "Fish! fish!" he cries. "It is fish!"[6]

Once again, Bilbo has been saved by "biased fortune" or "luck." It should be noted, however, that Gollum's own bad luck is his own fault. If he had behaved fairly and virtuously, giving Bilbo the little extra time for which Bilbo asked and which Gollum owed the hobbit in view of Bilbo's earlier granting of additional time to him, if, that is, he had not stepped from the boat in his uncharitable haste to claim his prize, Bilbo would never have received the saving hint. Gandalf's words that hatred often hurts itself and Theoden's epigram that "oft evil will shall evil mar" are proven correct yet again. The "biased fortune" is not only biased in favor of the virtuous, rewarding their merits, it is also biased against the wicked, allowing them to destroy themselves through their own malevolent actions.

Having answered Bilbo's next riddle, Gollum asks another hard riddle that has the hobbit flummoxed:

This thing all things devours:
Birds, beasts, trees, flowers;
Gnaws iron, bites steel;
Grinds hard stones to meal;
Slays king, ruins town,
And beats high mountain down.

For the second time, Gollum senses victory and, for the second time, his impatience gets the better of him. As Bilbo struggles for the solution, Gollum again gets out of his boat and paddles towards Bilbo. Hearing the splashing of his adversary's progress towards him but unable to see how far the creature is from him, the hobbit panics. He wants to shout out, "Give me more time! Give me time!" but his tongue seems to cleave to his palate and all that actually comes out, "with a sudden squeal," is "Time! Time!" Bilbo is saved by "pure luck," the narrator tells us, because "time" was of course the answer.[7] The hobbit is saved in the nick of time by a power beyond time itself but with the unwitting assistance of Gollum's own evil actions.

This particular riddle has a gravitas beyond the others because it resonates with a major theme of Tolkien's work, which is mortality, mutability, and the ravages of time. It also accentuates the Anglo-Saxon ambience of the riddles by evoking the melancholy musing of Old English poems, such as "The Ruin," "The Seafarer" or "The Wanderer," the last of which reminds us that "this middle earth each of all days ageth and falleth."[8] It further evokes the melancholy musing of Galadriel in *The Lord of the Rings* over "the long defeat" of Time, in which timeless virtue fights a tireless battle with the entropic decay of a Fallen cosmos.[9] Tolkien, echoing the voice of Galadriel, wrote in one of his letters that as "a Christian, and indeed a Roman Catholic, . . . I do not expect 'history' to be anything but a 'long defeat'—though it contains (and in a legend may contain more clearly and movingly) some samples or glimpses of final victory."[10] For the wise, therefore, such as Tolkien and Galadriel, human (or elvish) history is a long defeat against the ravages of time and evil, which contains glimpses of final victory for those with the eyes of faith and hope. Furthermore, in the legends that Tolkien creates, such as *The Hobbit* and *The Lord of the Rings*, those tantalizing glimpses of final victory can be seen "more clearly and movingly" through the "biased fortune" and "luck" which prevails against seemingly insurmountable odds.

The "luck" continues in the high-stakes game of riddling when Gollum, becoming angry and hungry in equal measure, does not go back to his boat as he had done previously but squats himself down in the dark right beside the frightened Bilbo. Gollum's presence, poking and pawing at him, prevents Bilbo from being able to think of another riddle. Gripping his sword more tightly with one hand and placing his other hand in his pocket, he is surprised to feel the Ring, which he had quite forgotten about. "What have I got in my pocket?' he says aloud, more as a question to himself at the sudden discovery of the forgotten Ring than anything addressed to Gollum. The miserable creature nonetheless takes the question as being addressed to him and complains, quite rightly, that the question is not fair because it is not a riddle. Bilbo, however, unable to think of anything else, sticks to his question, repeating it more

loudly and insistently. Gollum, presumably seeking just
compensation for the unfairness of the question, demands
three guesses. His first guess is "hands," which is only wrong
because Bilbo "had luckily just taken his hand out again."[11]

Having guessed incorrectly twice more, Gollum loses
the game. Bilbo demands that Gollum fulfill the terms of
their agreement by showing him the way out of the labyrinth. Gollum has no intention of keeping his promise
and decides to go back to the island on the lake to fetch
the Ring, which he believes is still there, not knowing that
he has lost it and that it is now in Bilbo's pocket. It is at
this point that the narrator tells us about the Ring's power
to make its wearer invisible. There is, however, an incongruous weakness in this part of the plot because Gollum
appears to want the Ring to help him kill Bilbo, whom he
is fearful of attacking because the hobbit is armed with a
sword. He believes that he will be safe if he wears the Ring
because Bilbo will not be able to see him. Since, however,
they are already in pitch darkness, with no light whatsoever
penetrating the subterranean gloom, what advantage would
there be in wearing the Ring? This glaring error aside, we
also discover at this time that the Ring causes the dragon
sickness in those who possess it, increasing its power over
them until they are possessed by it. Like one who is gripped
with an unwanted addiction, Gollum has long since ceased
to struggle against the Ring's hold over him. We learn that
he used to wear it until he tired of it, after which he wore
it in a pouch, "till it galled him." Finally he had taken to
hiding it in a hole in the rock on his island, but "was always
going back to look at it." Occasionally he still wore it, "when

he could not bear to be parted from it any longer"[12] or when hunger drove him into the torchlit realm of the goblins, hunting for orc-meat, at which point its power to render him invisible became very useful.

We also learn at this juncture, although only briefly and implicitly, about the Dark Lord who rules the Ring. The narrator mentions, in passing, "the Master who ruled them,"[13] in which *them* refers to Gollum and the Ring, indicating how those who become addicted to the Ring's power become slaves to the will of the Dark Lord. Although the name of Sauron is never mentioned in *The Hobbit*, we see in this passing reference to the mysterious "Master" and other references to "the Necromancer" that the larger epic was already germinating in Tolkien's imagination as he wrote the earlier work.

Discovering to his horror that the Ring is lost, Gollum soon guesses that the thing that Bilbo has in his pocket is his precious Ring. Enraged, he loses all fear of the hobbit's sword and is clearly intent on killing Bilbo in order to regain his lost possession. The hobbit flees in panic with Gollum in hot pursuit. Bilbo puts his hand in his pocket, and the Ring, which felt very cold, "quietly slipped on to his groping forefinger."[14] It's as though the Ring has put itself on, willing its way onto the hobbit's finger. Once again, insistently, we are reminded of Gandalf's words that Bilbo was *meant* to find the Ring. The Ring's Master wants it back and is using Bilbo as the unwitting agent to wrest it from Gollum's possession. And yet, as Gandalf surmises, "there was something else at work, beyond any design of the Ring-maker." On this deepest theological level, which Gandalf perceives, the Master of the Ring is himself an unwitting agent of the One God whom Tolkien in *The Silmarillion* calls Ilúvatar (the All-Father or Father-Of-All). Since this understanding of evil's ultimate subservience to the will of God is at the very heart of the "biased fortune" of *The Hobbit* and *The Lord of the Rings* it will serve us well to spend a little time understanding Tolkien's Christian theology as he expresses it in *The Silmarillion*.

In the Creation story, as told in *The Silmarillion*, Satan, who is known as Melkor, brings disharmony into the Great Music of God's Creation by weaving into it his own prideful themes. He desires that his will and not God's be done. God responds to Melkor's introduction of discordant themes into the Great Music by weaving them into new and majestically beautiful themes beyond Melkor's wildest imaginings: "And thou, Melkor, shalt see that no theme may be played that hath not its uttermost source in me, nor can any alter the music in my despite. For he that attempteth this shall prove but mine instrument in the devising of things more wonderful, which he himself hath not imagined."[15] These words of God to Satan in Tolkien's retelling of the Creation story help us to understand the "luck" and "biased fortune" that we see in Tolkien's work. Every evil design that is *meant* by the evil characters will ultimately serve the greater good that is *meant* by God. Bilbo is *meant* to find the Ring by the Ring's Master (Sauron) but at the same time he is *meant* to find it by the One God who is the ultimate Master of the Master. It is on this deepest level of what is *meant* that we discover the deepest *meaning* in *The Hobbit* and *The Lord of the Rings*.

Bilbo stumbles on, blinded by the dark, and not knowing that his wearing of the Ring has made him invisible. He
falls headlong and Gollum is upon him instantly; yet, aston-
ishingly, the enraged creature runs straight past him. The
Ring, in slipping itself onto Bilbo's finger, has saved itself
from falling into the hands of Gollum and, in so doing, has
saved the hobbit from almost certain death. Unwittingly, in
his pursuit of Bilbo, Gollum leads the hobbit, who is now
invisible and following on behind, to the way out of the labyrinth. Unprepared to go any further for fear of the goblins,
especially as he no longer has the cloak of invisibility, which
the wearing of the Ring supplied, Gollum squats down
miserably at the entrance, blocking Bilbo's exit. The hobbit
concludes that he must kill the creature in order to make
good his escape. He justifies this desperate measure because
of the desperate situation in which he finds himself and the
desperate need to escape from the subterranean prison, and
also from the fact that Gollum had clearly intended to kill
him. And yet his conscience troubles him. It would not be
a fair fight. He is invisible and has an unfair advantage. He
is also armed with a sword, whereas Gollum is unarmed.
Apart from these questions of fairness or justice, there is
also the question of pity or mercy towards Gollum, who is
"miserable, alone, lost":

A sudden understanding, a pity mixed with horror,
welled up in Bilbo's heart: a glimpse of endless unmarked
days without light or hope of betterment, hard stone, cold
fish, sneaking and whispering. All these thoughts passed in
a flash of a second.[16]

The moral and practical importance of this act of pity

and mercy is made clear by Gandalf, ever the voice of wisdom, in response to Frodo's exclamation in *The Lord of the Rings* that it was "a pity that Bilbo did not stab that vile creature, when he had the chance." "Pity?" Gandalf replies. "It was Pity that stayed his hand. Pity, and Mercy: not to strike without need. And he has been well rewarded, Frodo. Be sure that he took so little hurt from the evil, and escaped in the end, because he began his ownership of the Ring so. With Pity."[17] In these few words we see the distinction between the "biased fortune" of Providence, which is connected to the cooperation of the individual will, and the robotic determinism of Predestination, in which an individual is "saved" regardless of his willing participation in his salvation. Bilbo's escape was not predestined but was dependent, in part, on his own actions. It is only because he had behaved virtuously that he is ultimately able to escape. Although Gandalf appears to be referring to the long-term consequences of Bilbo's action, it is nonetheless implicit that Bilbo, if he had failed to act with pity and mercy, might have perished in the struggle with Gollum or that he might have been captured and killed by the goblins that he is soon to encounter. In choosing not to take Gollum's life, Bilbo unwittingly saved his own.

Returning to the long-term consequences of Bilbo's act of pity and mercy, Gandalf explains to Frodo that the fate of the whole quest to destroy the Ring depended on Bilbo's passing of this primary test of virtue: "My heart tells me that [Gollum] has some part to play yet, for good or ill, before the end: and when that comes, the pity of Bilbo may rule the fate of many—yours not least."[18] Gandalf's words are those of a prophet. When Frodo, on Mount Doom, fails through the power of his own will to overcome the more powerful evil of the Ring, he is saved by the timely intervention of Gollum, an intervention which would not have been possible if Bilbo had killed "that vile creature, when he had a chance." Thus we are reminded that not only do evil actions have consequences, but that acts of virtue have consequences also. The economy of grace that rules the cosmos ensures that virtue is ultimately rewarded as surely as it ensures that vice is ultimately punished.

Bilbo decides to leap over the squatting Gollum rather than kill him and his choice is rewarded instantly by another stroke of "luck" as, unknown to him in the darkness, "he only just missed cracking his skull on the low arch of the passage."[19] With the curses of Gollum fading behind him, he stumbles upon a group of goblins, no doubt roused by the echoing of Gollum's screams through the miles of tunnels. At this very moment, the Ring slips from Bilbo's finger, making him visible to the deadly foe. "Whether it was an accident, or a last trick of the ring before it took a new master, it was not on his finger."[20] Seeing this incident through the lens of the later work, we can't help but feel that this was the will of Sauron acting upon the Ring, intent on having the Ring delivered into the hands of orcs, from whom it would doubtless have found its way back to him. In the nick of time, Bilbo places the Ring back on his finger and manages to escape.

This single "last trick of the ring" is the almost last hint in *The Hobbit* of the ominous power that the Ring will wield in the later epic. As the adventure at hand unfolds, the role of the Ring is relegated to that of a mere tool which Bilbo will use with much success. It is for this reason, no doubt, that Tolkien uses the lower-case "ring" in *The Hobbit* whereas it is always rendered with the emphatic upper-case "Ring" in *The Lord of the Rings*. Following Tolkien's lead, we will now use the "ring" instead of the "Ring" as we continue to follow Bilbo on his quest to the Lonely Mountain.

CHAPTER 6

BILBO COMES OF AGE

THE MYSTICAL connection between virtuous choice and providential reward continues at the commencement of the following chapter in which Bilbo struggles with his own conscience as he decides whether he ought to go back into the goblin-infested tunnels to try to rescue his friends, especially as he now has the ring to render him invisible. Considering the horrific ordeal he has just gone through, one might have understood if fear and trembling got the better of him. He passes the test, however, and resolves to return to the perilous darkness, placing duty over desire, and thereby showing a willingness to lay down his life for his friends, which is the greatest love of all. Having resolved to die for his friends, if necessary, he is rewarded instantly when he hears their voices. They have also escaped from the deadly subterranean prison and he does not need to die just yet!

As Bilbo approaches, he hears Gandalf setting the same test to the dwarves that Bilbo himself had just passed. The wizard is insisting that they must go back into the tunnels to discover if Bilbo is still alive and, if he is, to try to rescue him. The dwarves are not convinced and blame Gandalf for his initial insistence that they bring the useless hobbit with them on the quest. When Bilbo emerges in their very midst, having removed the ring, they are all understandably surprised and not so sure that the hobbit is quite as "useless" as they'd supposed. On being asked how he escaped, he tells them that he "just crept along . . . very carefully and quietly" but omits saying anything about the ring.[1] On being pressed for more detail, he recounts the whole story of his adventure in the tunnels, "except about the finding of the ring ('not just now' he thought)."[2] Although this reluctance to divulge his finding of the ring might be seen as further evidence of the ring's dark power, it seems to have more to do with the dragon sickness, which re-emerges later in Bilbo's initial unwillingness to divulge his possession of the Arkenstone. The power of the ring and the dragon sickness are not unrelated, of course, both being rooted in a sinful desire for power, motivated by a prideful self-centeredness, but there is no suggestion that Sauron, or the Necromancer as he is known on the few passing occasions that he is mentioned in *The Hobbit*, is exerting his dark will over the ring and its wearer. On the contrary, the fact that Bilbo "just chuckled inside" when he first decides to keep the ring secret suggests that he thought it would be fun to have it as a trick up his sleeve, or in his pocket, of which the others are unaware. Such secrecy contains its own dangers but it appears harmless enough at this stage.

If Bilbo's secrecy about the ring does not necessarily indicate the ominous power of the ring itself, it does serve to show forth the true power of Gandalf. After Bilbo finishes telling his story, in every detail except that of the crucial role of the ring, Gandalf laughs and exclaims that "Mr Baggins has more about him than you guess." Gandalf's words are suggestive of his knowledge of the secret, a suggestion that is strengthened by Gandalf giving Bilbo "a queer look from under his bushy eyebrows, as he said this," causing the hobbit to wonder if the wizard had "guessed at the part of his tale that he had left out."[3] As Bilbo has not told Gandalf his secret, we must assume that the wizard guesses that the hobbit has a magic ring as the only explanation for his sudden and mysterious presence in their midst or, alternatively, that his knowledge has a preternatural source. If the latter, Gandalf can be said to possess a miraculous knowledge akin to that possessed by the Divine. Elsewhere, however, in both *The Hobbit* and *The Lord of the Rings*, it is clear that Gandalf does not possess Divine omniscience. He knows a great deal, and a great deal of what he knows he seems to know preternaturally, but he does not know everything. This level of knowledge is conducive to our understanding of angelic power, a supernatural power beyond that of men (or hobbits, dwarves, and elves) but below that of God Himself. Although these angelic qualities are never made explicit in either *The Hobbit* or *The Lord of the Rings* we know from Tolkien's wider legendarium that Gandalf is one of an order of angels known as the Istari. He is, therefore, not merely a wizard but a guardian angel, protecting Bilbo and the dwarves, and the whole of Middle-earth, from the dark power of the Enemy.

Gandalf's role is again made manifest some time later,

following another near fatal encounter with the goblins and a flight to safety with the Eagles, when he announces to the distraught dwarves and hobbit that he will soon be taking his leave of them: "I always meant to see you all safe (if possible) over the mountains, and now by good man-agement *and* good luck I have done it."[4] They have made it through the perilous Misty Mountains by a combination of his actions *and* "good luck," confirming the mystically dynamic interaction between free will (good management) and grace (good "luck").

Before leaving to attend to some urgent business of his own, which we learn about later, Gandalf introduces Bilbo and the dwarves to Beorn, a mysterious and threatening shape-changer, who can take the form of a man or a bear. He seems in some degree to manifest Tolkien's deep rever-ence for nature as God's Creation, serving as an image of Franciscan spirituality, much as Radagast the Brown does in *The Lord of the Rings*. Indeed, the connection between Beorn and Radagast is made explicit in *The Hobbit* when Gandalf introduces himself to Beorn as a cousin of Radagast. Beorn, who is not known for paying compliments, responds that Radagast is "not a bad fellow as wizards go" and that he "used to see him now and again."[5] Although Radagast does not make an appearance in *The Hobbit*, he is a neighbor of Beorn, residing in the Vales of Anduin, between Carrock and the Old Forest Road. These connections aside, the strongest links between Beorn, Radagast, and Franciscan spirituality are conveyed by Tolkien linguistically through their etymological relationship with each other.

Radagast means "tender of beasts" in Tolkien's

invented language of Adûnaic, and Radagast's original name, Aiwendil, means "bird-friend" in Tolkien's invented Quenya language, the latter of which, in particular, invokes a clear connection with St. Francis of Assisi. Like Beorn and St. Francis, Radagast has a strong and mystical love for wild beasts and for the flora and fauna of God's Creation. He speaks the tongues of birds, resonant of the legend of St. Francis' preaching to the birds, and he is described as a "master of shapes and changes of hue," resonant of Beorn the shape-changer. Radagast's simplicity causes the proud and sophisticated Saruman to dismiss him scornfully as "Radagast the Bird-tamer! Radagast the Simple! Radagast the Fool!,"[6] much as the proud and sophisticated people of thirteenth century Italy dismissed St. Francis. The saint seemed unfazed by the insults, considering himself a *jongleur de Dieu* (God's juggler or God's tumbler) and a fool for Christ.

The etymological connections to Beorn's name are equally intriguing and display Tolkien's profound knowledge of the ancient languages of northern Europe. Whereas *Beorn* means "man" or "warrior" in Old English, *bjorn* means "bear" in Old Norse. In Old Norse literature, "The Saga of Hrolf Kraki" features a character named Beorn who, like his namesake in *The Hobbit*, could change his shape into the form of a bear. Beorn also has ties to the Old English epic, *Beowulf*. In Old English, *beo* means "bee" and *wulf* means "wolf." Beowulf's name, therefore, means "bee's wolf" or "bee-wolf," a euphemistic name for a bear as a "honey-eater."[7] Beorn, who keeps bees, lives simply, and is at one with nature, is, therefore, a cross between the simple and peaceful "Franciscan" Radagast, and the fearsome war-riors of Old English epics and Old Norse sagas. The former is to the fore in the way in which Beorn grows drowsy and pays little attention when the dwarves discuss their love of gold, silver, and jewels "and the making of things by smith-craft." We are told that Beorn "did not appear to care for such things: there were no gold or silver in his hall, and few save the knives were made of metal at all."[8] It is clear that Beorn, in his Franciscan simplicity, is never likely to fall foul of the dragon sickness to which the dwarves will soon prove themselves all too susceptible.

Perhaps the most enigmatic dimension to Beorn's role within *The Hobbit* is the way in which he seems to emerge almost as a metaphor of Gandalf's role in the story as a father-figure and as a guardian of Bilbo and the dwarves. As Gandalf accompanies the hobbit and his dwarf compan-ions to the edge of Mirkwood, he reminds them that they must release the ponies that Beorn had lent them before entering the forest. When the dwarves grumble at having to relinquish their beasts of burden, Gandalf tells them that "Beorn is not as far off as you seem to think, and you had better keep your promises." Although the dwarves can-not see him, Gandalf tells them that Beorn, in bear shape, had followed them every night and had sat watching their camps as they slept. This was "to guard you and guide you" but also to ensure that they kept their promise to return the ponies to him. It is now that Gandalf finally announces that it is time for him to leave them so that he can attend to "some pressing business away south."[9] Although we can-not doubt that Gandalf does have "pressing business away south," especially as Mordor lies in that direction, we can't help feeling that, like Beorn, he will remain in some sense a guardian and guide, out of sight but never too far that he won't arrive when he is most needed. Indeed, we sense that Bilbo and the dwarves had better heed his words and keep their promises or else suffer very unpleasant consequences.

Gandalf's parting advice to them is that their success will depend "on your luck and on your courage and sense." We already know that "luck" is a euphemism for the presence of a providence that rewards virtue and punishes vice, whereas the necessity of courage and sense indicates the role of free will to the success or failure of the quest. Nothing is guaranteed. The future depends on faith and hope in the power of providence combined with virtuous action. On the other hand, a fall into folly could lead to failure. Further evidence of Gandalf's prophetic powers are seen in his reminder to the dwarves that he is sending Bilbo with them: "I have told you before that he has more about him than you guess, and you will find that out before long."[10]

After Bilbo asks whether there is some other way of getting to the Lonely Mountain without facing the darkness and peril of Mirkwood, Gandalf tells him that the Grey Mountains to the north are crawling with "orcs of the worst description" and that to the south lies "the land of the Necromancer: and even you, Bilbo, won't need me to tell you tales of that black sorcerer. I don't advise you to go anywhere near the places overlooked by his dark tower!"[11] We won't need reminding that Gandalf has just announced that he is himself heading south and our imaginative appetites can't help but be whetted with curiosity with regard

to the nature of the "business" that Gandalf might have
with Sauron, the Necromancer, in the shadow of the dark
tower. Within a few years, Tolkien would satisfy our whetted appetites, weaving a tale about Gandalf's war with the
Necromancer and the Shadow he casts in a way and on a
scale that is barely hinted at in the earlier book. For the time
being, however, we are told no more. Instead we are left
only with Gandalf's last words of advice before he departs:
"Stick to the forest track, keep your spirits up, hope for the
best, and with a tremendous slice of luck you *may* come out
one day and see the Long Marshes lying below you . . ."[12] In
effect, the wizard tells them to proceed with faith and hope,
but he warns that they will still need a miracle to survive
the experience. It's no wonder that Thorin growls disconso-
lately at the cold comfort being offered. Gandalf's very last
words are unequivocal and could not be starker or plainer:
"Be good, take care of yourselves—and DON'T LEAVE
THE PATH!" Here we see Gandalf as the archetypal father-
figure advising his children as they embark on a journey
on which he cannot be present to watch over them that
they should *be good, be careful, and don't do anything stupid!* The advice is, however, charged with Christian moral
guidance, which the everyday language might obscure if we
are not paying due attention. Being good, i.e. virtuous, is
the prerequisite for success, whereas taking care implies the
need to practice the cardinal virtues of prudence and temperance. Most importantly, the emphatic exhortation that
they should not, under any circumstances, leave the path
reminds the Christian of the words of Christ: *Enter ye in at
the narrow gate: for wide is the gate, and broad is the way that*

leadeth to destruction, and many there are who go in thereat.
(Matthew 7:13)

In spite of such emphatic and unequivocal advice, Bilbo
and the dwarves are tempted to leave the path as soon as
the pinch of hunger begins to hurt and as soon as the sound
of elven feasting in the distance, lit by a welcoming light,
beckons them. Although Thorin reminds them that a feast
will do them no good, "if we never got back alive from it,"
the lure of hunger and the allure of the elven festivities
prove too strong. The prospect of full stomachs overcomes
the qualms of prudence or temperance and, ignoring the
wizard's warnings, "they all left the path and plunged into
the forest together."[13] Before long, they are hopelessly lost in
the darkness of the forest and Bilbo finds himself separated
from the rest of the party. He is attacked by a giant spider
and is forced to defend himself. He strikes the spider in its
eyes with his sword and, with a further stroke of his blade,
kills it. "Somehow the killing of the giant spider, all alone
by himself in the dark without the help of the wizard or
the dwarves or of anyone else, made a great difference to
Mr Baggins. He felt a different person, and much fiercer
and bolder in spite of an empty stomach, as he wiped his
sword on the grass and put it back into its sheath."[14] This
is Bilbo's initiation into the world of the warrior and, as a
mark of its importance and its defining character, the hobbit baptizes the moment by giving his sword the name
of *Sting*. He has come of age. He has become something
more than he was before. He has grown-up. The vanquishing of the monster, all alone in the dark without the help
of the wizard, was a rite of passage. Perhaps, we begin to

surmise, this was at least part of the reason for Gandalf's departure.

As the dim grey light of morning breaks through the canopy of trees, Bilbo sets out to find his companions. He makes a guess at the direction from which he last heard their cries—"and by luck . . . guessed more or less right."[15] Although his own "luck" is still with him, he soon discovers that the luck of the dwarves appears to have deserted them. He discovers them hanging in cocoons spun by the giant spiders, still alive but ready to be eaten, a grim foreshadowing of Frodo's encounter with Shelob in *The Lord of the Rings*. With the use of the ring and his wits he manages to lure the spiders away from their prey and doubles back to free the dwarves from their spider-spun shrouds. Never again will the dwarves doubt Gandalf's promise that the hobbit would prove invaluable to their quest!

Having survived the ghoulish prospect of being eaten alive by monstrous spiders, Bilbo and the dwarves face the less gruesome but equally perilous prospect of starving to death in the forest. Seemingly doomed to wander in a forlorn hope of finding the path, they are saved from starvation by a company of wood elves who take them prisoner, all, that is, except Bilbo who puts on the ring and follows the party to the Elvenking's palace. The dwarves are all imprisoned and it is Bilbo, once again, who saves the day, with the help of his trusty ring. As Bilbo serves as the invisible messenger, enabling the imprisoned Thorin to pass messages to the other dwarves in their respective cells around the palace, the dwarf-leader places all his trust in the hobbit. With renewed hope, Thorin decides not to ransom himself with a promise to the Elvenking of a share in the dragon's treasure until all hope of escaping in any other way are exhausted, "until in fact the remarkable Mr Invisible Baggins (of whom he began to have a very high opinion indeed) had altogether failed to think of something clever."[16] Thorin's esteem for the hobbit was shared equally by the other dwarves. "[T]hey all trusted Bilbo. Just what Gandalf had said would happen, you see. Perhaps that was part of his reason for going off and leaving them."[17]

If we hadn't guessed as much already, the narrator spells it out for us. We "see," as he means us to see, that Gandalf's departure was necessary for Bilbo to finally come of age, and that it is likely that Gandalf knew it and meant it as at least part of his reason for leaving. Gandalf realizes, as all fathers and other guardians must, that the bird can only become fully what it is meant to be by being made to fly the nest.

Let's pause for a moment, lest the reader's imagination runs wild with the idea that being let loose is necessarily the same as going astray. In the story, Bilbo and the dwarves go astray by failing to follow their guardian's commandment to keep to the narrow path. Furthermore, their going astray very nearly proves fatal. Going astray is not good. It is not to be encouraged. Indeed it is to be actively discouraged. In fact, it should be forbidden by sensible and sagacious commandments! Nonetheless, just as God Himself gave our first parents the freedom to go astray by giving them freedom itself, we must let our own little hobbits loose so that they can learn the lessons that life must teach if they are to grow into the fullness of whom they are meant to be.

Gandalf, as a model of true guardianship, accompanies the hobbit and the dwarves on their journey for as long as is necessary. Until they reach the maturity required to defeat the evils that their journey will throw at them, the guardian remains at their side to protect them and to vanquish their foes. At the same time, he teaches them with his words and his example, conveying in his actions the wisdom and virtue necessary to fly the nest without falling to their deaths. The raising of birds or hobbits (or people) is about teaching them to fly without falling. Gandalf does not leave too soon but he leaves soon enough for the lessons to be learned. He flies the nest himself, leaving his charges to their own devices, to force them, at the right moment, to fly the nest as well. If he is not there to do their fighting for them they must learn to survive on their own. They must fly or fall. And yet, of course, they are never fully on their own. There is always "luck." With the right disposition, one trusts in the "luck" that is necessary as the correlative of virtuous action.

This aspect of the Christian moral vision of *The Hobbit* is shared by *The Lord of the Rings* as was perceived with critical insight by the British journalist, Paul Goodman, who, responding to shallow and negative criticism of Tolkien's work, wrote of the latter work that the "circular journey from the Shire to Mordor and back to the Shire again is all about growing older—or, rather, about growing up." Furthermore, Goodman continued, the various aspects of the book's plot "all point to conclusions as true as they are commonplace: that growing up is painful, but cannot be avoided; that it involves hard choices, which we are free to take; that choices have consequences, and that even good ones will not bring back the past."[18] Goodman's perception of the deepest meaning of Tolkien's work was informed by his understanding that "the key" to *The Lord of the Rings* was its "religious sensibility," an understanding which is lacking in too many of Tolkien's critics.

The irony is not merely that Tolkien's critics lack the necessary religious sensibility to understand *The Hobbit* and *The Lord of the Rings* but that they are simply not mature enough. They fail to perceive that the books are about growing-up because they are not really grown-ups themselves. Lacking the necessary maturity, they fail to see that the books serve to remind us that growing up is about growing in wisdom and virtue and learning to curtail our selfishness so that we can give ourselves more selflessly to others. This is a lesson that modern adults need to learn because many of them have forgotten the very meaning of adulthood, as is evident in the adulteration of the meaning of adulthood by the language-debasers. If we take the meaning of "adult" to mean "grown-up" or "mature" we can state categorically that there is nothing adult about "adult" bookstores, websites, or movies, for example. Pornography is not grown-up; it is adolescent. It shows a lack of maturity, an unwillingness to grow in virtue and to struggle against concupiscence.

The world needs love—not the "love" on offer at "adult" bookstores but the real, self-sacrificial love which lays down its life for its friends. What the world needs is the truly adult love which is fulfilled in true marriage and the parenthood which is its purpose. The best way of becoming a grown-up is to become a parent in a real marriage between a man and woman who sacrifice themselves for each other and for their children. Ironically, considering the absence of marriage or children in the story, this is the love that we find in *The Hobbit*. It is a love which shows us not only how to be good adults but how to be good husbands, wives and parents. It shows us that what the world needs now are grown-ups like Bilbo, not fake "adults."

This tangential aside about the meaning of adulthood helps us to focus on one of the main reasons for the importance of *The Hobbit* and *The Lord of the Rings* and one of the principal reasons for their being misunderstood by modern critics. As with Frodo in the later book, Bilbo in *The Hobbit* is in some ways an Everyman figure who shows us ourselves or, perhaps more importantly, shows us who we ought to be. *The Hobbit* calls all of its readers to grow-up. This is a lesson that is important for children but is equally important for "adults" who are having difficulty being grown-up. Bilbo's tests of virtue are as applicable to his readers on their journey through life as they are applicable to Bilbo himself. His journey is our journey and the lessons that he learns are lessons that we are also meant to learn. As Gandalf might say to each of us, *I can put it no plainer than by saying that Bilbo is* meant *to grow-up and that you are* meant *to grow-up also.*

CHAPTER 7

THE RETURN OF THE KING

AFTER BILBO steals the key from the drunken and
sleeping chief guard, and after releasing the imprisoned dwarves with it, he "kind-heartedly" puts the keys
back on the chief guard's belt in the hope that it will allevi-
ate the trouble the guard will face following the discovery
of the escaped prisoners.[1] The prisoners make their getaway
concealed in empty barrels, with the exception of Bilbo who
leaps into the water wearing the ring and travels down-
stream, floating on one of the barrels. The barrels are being
floated downriver to be collected and taken to Lake-town
for re-use. As "luck" would have it, this method of escape
is also the only practical method of reaching their destina-
tion. The little known track they'd been following through
Mirkwood came "to a doubtful and little used end at the
eastern edge of the forest."[2] Even if Bilbo and the dwarves
had managed to make their way through Mirkwood by
the path, they'd have found themselves lost in seemingly
impassable marshes and bogs. The Forest River on which
they are travelling is the only safe way to get from the edge

of the forest to the plains beyond. "So you see," the narrator tells us, "Bilbo had come in the end by the only road that was any good."[3]

The "road" leads straight to Lake-town. Upon their arrival, though they look hungry and disheveled after the arduous and claustrophobic nature of their journey from the elven palace, Thorin and his company of dwarves are treated like kings by the common people. This is not surprising because their return was prophesied in legends that had become folklore. Thorin had spoken magical words into the ears of those who heard when he declared himself to be "Thorin son of Thrain son of Thror King under the Mountain! I have come back."[4] As news spreads of the legendary king's return, the people of Lake-town begin to sing old songs concerning the return of the King under the Mountain:

> *The King beneath the mountains,*
>> *The King of carven stone,*
> *The lord of silver fountains*
>> *Shall come into his own!*
>
> *His crown shall be upholden,*
>> *His harp shall be restrung,*
> *His halls shall echo golden*
>> *To songs of yore re-sung.*
>
> *The woods shall wave on mountains*
>> *And grass beneath the sun;*
> *His wealth shall flow in fountains*
>> *And the rivers golden run.*

The streams shall run in gladness,
  The lakes shall shine and burn,
All sorrow fail and sadness
  At the Mountain-king's return![5]

Clearly there is a potent and palpable parallel between *The Hobbit* and *The Lord of the Rings* in this shared theme of the return of the king. And yet, apart from their shared kingship and the fact that both kings return from exile to claim their rightful inheritance, it seems that Aragorn and Thorin could not be more different. Aragorn's character and kingship are marked not only with great courage and martial prowess but with meekness and humility and, ultimately, with the miraculous and Christ-like healing power that he shows in the Paths of the Dead and the Houses of Healing. Thorin, by comparison, is grumpy and obstreperous and falls into the destructive dragon sickness. Aragorn appears to be a paragon of kingly virtue, worthy of respect, reverence, and emulation; Thorin, on the other hand, seems tainted by pride and greed, and serves as a cautionary image of vice and its harmful consequences. Such differences should not, however, distract us from the importance of kingship, nor from the importance of the king's return, which is clearly a matter for rejoicing in both books.

Tolkien, as a Catholic and as a medievalist, drew deep draughts of inspiration from his understanding of true kingship, particularly as manifested by legendary and historical examples of exiled kings who return to claim their rightful inheritance. The first example of kingship, at least as it relates to Aragorn's coronation in *The Lord of the Rings*, is the figure of Charlemagne (Charles the Great), the first Holy Roman Emperor. Charlemagne, as the true king, unites all the people of Christendom, as Aragorn unites all the free peoples of Middle-earth.

Another figure who looms large inspirationally on the theme of returned kingship in *The Hobbit* and *The Lord of the Rings* is that of King Arthur and the Arthurian legends that surround him. Arthur is the once and future king of popular legend who hasn't really died but is only sleeping. He will return, so it is believed, in a time of great peril to deliver England from her enemies. The idea of the once and future king resonates with the person of Aragorn, the descendant of an ancient royal line who returns as a long-lost and almost forgotten king to claim his rightful inheritance and to save his kingdom from the grip of evil. Thorin, though a pale shadow of both Arthur and Aragorn, is clearly made in the Arthurian mould in the sense that his return is heralded by such rejoicing by the common folk of Lake-land.

The other aspect of kingship that manifests Tolkien's understanding of English history from a Catholic perspective is that of the Jacobite king-in-exile. Jacobites remain loyal to the true king of England, James II, a Catholic, who was forced into exile by the so-called Glorious Revolution of 1688. This Revolution, far from being "glorious," was, in fact, a *coup d'état* in which an army of foreign mercenaries invaded the country, financed by wealthy anti-Catholic nobility, bankers and merchants, to overthrow the power of the true king. The king was forced into exile. He raised an army to attempt to reclaim the throne but was defeated in

Ireland. In the eighteenth century there were two Jacobite uprisings in which the descendants of the true king endeavored to reclaim the throne. The second uprising, led by James' legitimate heir, Bonnie Prince Charlie, was crushed at the battle of Culloden in 1746. Ever since this decisive defeat, Jacobites have lamented the passing of the Catholic monarchy, believing that the present incumbent on the throne is either a usurper, at worst, or a steward who is keeping the throne warm, so to speak, until the true king in exile returns. As a devout Catholic who was steeped in the history of England, Tolkien understood all of this, and there are obvious parallels between the way that a Jacobite would view the legal status of the present Royal Family and the status of Denethor as the Steward of Gondor in *The Lord of the Rings*. From a Jacobite perspective, Queen Elizabeth II and Denethor are both *de facto* rulers who hold the throne until the return of the *de jure* ruler, the True King. For a Jacobite, therefore, and it is safe to assume that Tolkien had Jacobite sympathies, the return of Aragorn would have resonated with particular poignancy. We are reminded again, perhaps, of Tolkien's lament that, as "a Christian, and indeed a Roman Catholic . . . I do not expect 'history' to be anything but a 'long defeat'—though it contains (and in a legend may contain more clearly and movingly) some samples or glimpses of final victory."[6] In his own legend, Tolkien shows us such a glimpse in Aragorn's triumphant return.

By comparison, Thorin is certainly a pathetic figure but his true kingship is not in doubt, nor is the joy of the people at his prophesied return. Like Aragorn, he has come to reclaim that which is rightfully his. The dragon, Smaug, the enemy which Thorin must defeat, is a usurper who is squatting illegitimately on the "throne" of Thorin's kingdom, claiming its gold, silver, and jewels as his own. Having no legitimate right to the riches of the true king's realm, the dragon has seized it by force. There he squats, Smaug the Smug, confident in possession of his ill-gotten gains and heedless of the songs that men sing about the return of the king. It is clear, therefore, in the lesser of Tolkien's two tales as much as in the greater, that the Jacobite theme is as present and that the return of the king is as necessary for the restoration of justice.

Before we continue with the events surrounding Thorin's return and the story of Bilbo's pilgrimage, it is important to remind ourselves that kingship itself is only legitimate insofar as it holds its authority from God. All true kings are only true insofar as they reflect the True Kingship of Christ. We shall see soon enough whether Thorin is true to his kingship but, as for Aragorn, Tolkien shows us that his true power comes from his being a true image of Christ the King. All lesser images, such as Aragorn's connection to Charlemagne, Arthur, or the Jacobite kings-in-exile, fall into shadow in the presence of Christ's Kingship which Aragorn's kingship reflects. In this ultimate and highest sense of Kingship, the return of the king signifies the Second Coming when the "long defeat" of history will be vanquished by the final victory of Christ. This is the ultimate return from exile of the True King to claim his own.

As with Christ, Aragorn's true kingship is revealed in his miraculous ability to heal the sick. "The hands of the king are the hands of a healer," says the wise-woman of Gondor, "and so shall the rightful king be known."[7] Apart from the obvious references to the healing powers of Christ in the Gospel, Tolkien's love for Anglo-Saxon England would have made him well aware of the Anglo-Saxon king, St. Edward the Confessor, who was known to have such miraculous powers of healing, a fact to which Shakespeare alludes in *Macbeth*, in which the true kingship of Edward the Confessor is contrasted with the murderous Machiavellianism of Macbeth. Finally, like Christ, Aragorn's power of healing extends not only to the living, but also to the dead. When he takes the Paths of the Dead, he reveals that he has the power to release the dead from their curse. This is an inescapable reminder of Christ's descent into hell following the Crucifixion and His liberation of the dead from Limbo.

We can expect no such miracles from the flawed and ambitious King Thorin. Yet, as the narrator reminds us, the Master of Lake-town is wrong in his cynical belief that Thorin and his dwarf-companions are frauds who will never actually dare to go anywhere near the Lonely Mountain and its terrifying dragon: "He was wrong. Thorin, of course, was really the grandson of the King under the Mountain, and there is no knowing what a dwarf will not dare and do for revenge or the recovery of his own."[8] Like Aragorn, Thorin has legitimacy on his side. He is indeed the true king. Unlike Aragorn, he does not return to save his people but to "recover his own." Nor does he return with Aragorn's meekness and humility but with a pride that will do or dare anything for revenge. Aragorn is exalted in his humility and, as we shall see, Thorin will be humbled in his pride.

CHAPTER 8

ABOVE ALL SHADOWS
RIDES THE SUN

A S THE unfolding of the plot reveals, dragon sickness is not restricted to dragons. Apart from Bilbo's own affliction with it, the dwarves are clearly driven by their desire to regain the treasure and Thorin becomes utterly possessed by his obsession with hoarding it for himself once the dragon is slain. His heart is poisoned by his possessive gold-lust and he forgets his friendship with Bilbo, and the debt that he owes to him, in the hardness and blindness which the dragon sickness causes. Clearly, therefore, the theme of the dragon sickness forms an integral part of the work, especially during the story's climactic denouement. As we approach this climax, the characterization of the Master of Lake-town serves as a prophetic prelude to the emergent theme. From his first appearance we see that he is afflicted with the dragon sickness and the blindness it causes. He does not believe in legends and has little time for folklore and tradition. He doesn't think much of the "old songs" that the people are singing about the portentous return of the king, "giving his mind to trade and tolls, to cargo and gold, to which habit he owed his position."[1] In consequence, the Master is not sorry to see the departure of Bilbo and the dwarves, believing that Smaug will destroy them and that he will be rid of the inconvenience that they have already caused him: "They were expensive to keep, and their arrival had turned things into a long holiday in which business was at a standstill."[2]

The mounting tension that Bilbo, Thorin, *et al* feel as they initially approach the Lonely Mountain dissipates into a sense of frustration and futility as they fail to find the promised access to the Dragon's lair. The dwarves begin to despair of ever finding a way of opening the hidden door to Smaug's cave. Dwalin laments that "our beards will grow till they hang down the cliff to the valley before anything happens here."[3] Bilbo is the only one who retains any hope of redemption from their apparently hopeless situation. As the others wander aimlessly, Bilbo sits on the doorstep staring at the stone which sat immovably where the door should be or else gazing into the distant west. He has a "queer feeling" that he is waiting for something and hopes that perhaps Gandalf will suddenly return to save the day. As he gazes westward he notices the sun beginning to set on the distant horizon and also a new moon, pale in the sky. At that very moment he hears a sharp crack behind him and sees a large thrush knocking a snail on the stone. Astonished, he realizes that the prophecy revealed by the moon-letters is coming true: *Stand by the grey stone when the thrush knocks and the setting sun with the last light of Durin's Day will shine upon the key-hole.* Remembering Thorin's explanation that

Durin's Day only occurs on "the first day of the last moon of Autumn on the threshold of Winter . . . when the last moon of Autumn and the sun are in the sky together,"[4] Bilbo calls to the dwarves to come and witness the imminent miracle. The dwarves wait with growing impatience, their hopes sinking with the setting sun, but Bilbo, with faith, hope, and confidence in the miracle about to be revealed, waits with quiet patience. "Then suddenly when their hope was lowest a red ray of the sun escaped like a finger through a rent in the cloud. A gleam of light came straight through the opening into the bay and fell on the smooth rock-face . . . There was a loud crack. A flake of rock split from the wall and fell. A hole appeared suddenly about three feet from the ground."[5] In a few breathless moments, Thorin draws the key from round his neck and places it in the hole. "It fitted and it turned! Snap! The gleam went out, the sun sank, the moon was gone, and evening sprang into the sky."[6] The party had gained miraculous access to the treasure vault under the mountain by opening a safe, protected by Providence, which could only be opened by a divinely ordained combination.

One might be tempted to see in the finger of sunlight touching the stone and revealing its secret a symbolic reflection of the most famous finger in all of art, that of God Himself, touching the fingertip of Adam in Michelangelo's fresco on the ceiling of the Sistine Chapel. Clearly the finger of God is present in both as the miraculous source of light, life, and ultimate salvation. For those familiar with *The Lord of the Rings* it is also reminiscent of a similar scene at the Cross-roads of Ithilian, shortly before Frodo, Sam, and Gollum ascend the perilous Stairs of Cirith Ungol. At the Cross-roads they come across the seated statue of an old king, gnawed with age and maimed by the violent hands of orcs. It was headless and had been covered with the obscene graffiti of the maggot-folk of Mordor. On its headless shoulders had been placed a rough-hewn stone, which had been "rudely painted by savage hands in the likeness of a grinning face with one large red eye in the midst of its forehead."[7] The vandalization of the statue and the placing of the symbol of Sauron on its shoulders seem symbolic of the apparently hopeless situation in which Frodo and Sam find themselves and symbolic too, perhaps, of the final triumph of evil. Suddenly, the level rays of the setting sun illuminate the discarded head of the statue. "Look!" Frodo cries. "The king has got a crown again!"

The eyes were hollow and the carven beard was broken, but about the high stern forehead there was a coronal of silver and gold. A trailing plant with flowers like small white stars had bound itself across the brows as in reverence for the fallen king, and in the crevices of his stony hair yellow stonecrop gleamed.

"They cannot conquer forever!" said Frodo. And then suddenly the brief glimpse was gone. The Sun dipped and vanished, and as if at the shuttering of a lamp, black night fell.[8]

In this scene, as in the scene on the Lonely Mountain, the rays of the setting sun serve as the finger of God, touching a seemingly desperate moment with the providential promise of hope's fulfillment. And yet the scene from *The Lord of the Rings* is more subtle because it is more believable on an agnostic level of mere coincidence. The correlation of sunlight illuminating the beauty of flowers on a stone ruin is something that anyone might see. The sudden revelation that Frodo and Sam receive could be simply a coincidence of nature and could be dismissed as such. Indeed, a skeptic might see Frodo's symbolic connection of the statue's "crowning" with the return of the king and the defeat of Sauron as, at best, poetic wishful thinking, or, at worst, mere superstition. In fact, however, we know that Frodo's "wishful thinking" comes true, not because of a lucky coincidence, the product of mere chance, but because he has the "luck" of Providence on his side. Thus, when Sam, in a similarly desperate moment, sings the line "above all shadows rides the Sun,"[9] we know that the Sun is not merely the sun, any more than the Shadow is merely a shadow, but that the Sun is symbolic of the presence of a light that the darkness cannot penetrate. It is, as Tolkien's friend Roy Campbell proclaimed in his sonnet, "To the Sun," a light that both reveals and conceals the Light which is its source:

> Oh let your shining orb grow dim,
> Of Christ the mirror and the shield,
> That I may gaze through you to Him,
> See half the miracle revealed . . .[10]

It is also, according to the poet Charles Causley, not merely a mirror of Christ, reflecting His Divine Presence, but a title that Christ claims as his own:

> I am the great sun, but you do not see me,
> I am your husband, but you turn away . . .

> I am your wife, your child, but you will
>   leave me,
> I am that God to whom you will not pray.[11]

In the same way, the presence of the sun in Middle-earth is often a signifier of the hidden hand of God, the guarantor that the Divine Light rides above all shadows and that it overrides the designs of the Dark Lord or the Dragon. It offers "the glimpse of final victory" to which Tolkien refers in the letter quoted on page [69–].[12] Compare Tolkien's reference to this *glimpse* of victory with the passage from *The Lord of the Rings* that we've just highlighted: *"They cannot conquer forever!" said Frodo. And then suddenly the brief* glimpse *was gone. The Sun dipped and vanished . . .*

This employment of the Sun as signifying a *glimpse* or *gleam* of the Divine presence is further illustrated by a passage from Tolkien's celebrated essay "On Fairy Stories": "The peculiar quality of the 'joy' in successful Fantasy can thus be explained as a sudden *glimpse* of the underlying reality or truth . . . a far-off *gleam* or echo of *evangelium* in the real world . . ."[13] Compare this with the passage from *The Hobbit*, which begins and ends with the "far-off gleam" of the Sun: *Then suddenly when their hope was lowest a red ray of the sun escaped like a finger through a rent in the cloud. A* gleam *of light came straight through the opening . . . The* gleam *went out, the sun sank . . .*

As we ponder the importance of the Sun as a symbol of the presence of Divine light and life in the world, we might see its absence as symbolic of the Shadow of evil and also of the dragon sickness which is its consequence. Those who refuse to see the glimpses of Providence and ignore the gleam of *evangelium* are condemning themselves to a world of shadow in which the light is eclipsed by the darkness of sin. With this sobering thought in mind, it is time to meet the Dragon.

CHAPTER 9

Dragon Sickness

H AVING GAINED access to the secret passage to the dragon's den, Thorin reminds Bilbo that the time has come for him to "perform the service" for which he was included in their company and to "earn his Reward."[1] Bilbo is angered by Thorin's suggestion and the pompous tone in which it is made and reminds him and the other dwarves that he has already saved them from being eaten alive by the giant spiders and from incarceration in the palace of the elven king, neither of which were in the original bargain. Considering the "services" he has already rendered to the company, he suggests that he is "already owed some reward."[2] Nonetheless, and with a gesture of heroic magnanimity, he agrees to explore the secret passage, even though none of the dwarves agree to go with him.

Slipping the ring onto his finger and creeping down into the depths of the tunnel, he is trembling with fear and yet resolute. Bilbo is clearly "a very different hobbit"[3] from the one who had left the Shire so reluctantly months earlier. Going "down, down, down into the dark"[4] he discovers at last the dragon's den. "To say that Bilbo's breath was taken away is no description at all. There are no words left to express his staggerment, since Men changed the language that they learned of elves in the days when all the world was wonderful."[5] This is not the place to take a long tangential diversion to explore the linguistic ramifications of these words of the narrator, but suffice it to say that Tolkien, as a philologist, perceived that language, the very vehicle with which we think and communicate, is in the process of decay. If language, the tool that we need to perceive reality, is decaying or regressing, it throws into question the whole notion of "progress." If modern English is a dumbed-down and decadent form of that spoken by our ancestors, whether it be the Old English of the Anglo-Saxons, which Tolkien loved, or the Early Modern English of Shakespeare, how can we engage intellectually with the cosmos we experience as well as our ancestors did, or communicate that engagement to others? We are constrained within a linguistic straitjacket that continues to shrink, or, to employ the language that the Anglo-Saxons might have used, our word-horde is being depleted. Whether this entropic decay is unavoidable and unassailable, or whether it is the consequence of disenchantment, and therefore reversible through re-enchantment, is an interesting and vitally important question. It is, however, beyond the bounds of our present pursuit of Bilbo on his pilgrimage.

Bilbo's "staggerment" is caused by his first sight of the sleeping Smaug, his "wings folded like an immeasurable bat"[6] and his belly encrusted with gold and bejeweled with gems from his long lying on the mountain of treasure which serves as his bed and as the center of his world. Apart from gold and gems in immense quantity, the walls of the dragon's den are adorned with coats of mail, swords, spears, helms, and axes. The wonderful treasure trove and the dreadful dragon sleeping in its midst fills the hobbit with a simultaneous sensation of utter wonder and unutterable terror. Overcoming his fear, he steals forward to the edge of the mountain of treasure and takes a large two-handled cup from under the nostrils of the sleeping monster.

Bilbo retreats up the tunnel carrying his prize and shows it to the delighted dwarves. They scarcely have time to celebrate the liberation of the first piece of treasure before they are reminded of the difficulty they will face in liberating any more of it. Smaug awakens and discovers that one of his precious possessions is missing. His fury erupts like a volcano from the depths of the mountains. We are told that dragons have no real use for all their wealth, "but they know it to an ounce as a rule, especially after long possession."[7] As with the "clever" inventions of the orcs, which we discussed earlier, the obsessive possessiveness of dragons is applicable to people whom we might know in our own lives, or perhaps it might even be applicable to ourselves. The dragon sickness is a euphemism for the bourgeois materialism which is rife in our consumerist culture. Smaug's fury at the loss of a single insignificant and practically useless trinket serves as a metaphor for modern man and his mania for possessing trash that he doesn't need. As if to make sure that we don't miss the applicable point, the narrator tells us on the following page that Smaug's rage "passes description—the sort

of rage that is only seen when rich folk that have more than
they can enjoy suddenly lose something that they have long
had but have never before used or wanted."[8]

There is, however, a danger in seeing the dragon as
a metaphor for man, especially if the metaphor is a mere
manifestation of a human attribute. It is a danger which is
rooted in anthropocentrism and the materialism it spawns.
For Tolkien, dragons are not mere figments of the imagination, still less are they mere figments of the imagination
that are conjured for the sole purpose of teaching allegorical lessons. On the contrary, imaginary dragons are
found in his story because real dragons are found in history. Real dragons are not like dinosaurs, which are purely
natural creatures, such as whales or elephants, but preternatural creatures like angels or demons. In fact, dragons
in Christian iconography and Christian legend are always
demonic. They are never merely big, like a tyrannosaurus
rex, but are evil, like the devil himself. Thus, depictions in
art of St. Michael's vanquishing of the devil often portray
Satan as dragon-like. Similarly the story of St. George and
the Dragon is ultimately about the saint's conquest of Satan,
not about a noble warrior's conquest of a large and dangerous beast.

For Christians, and let's not forget that Tolkien was a
lifelong practicing Catholic, the devil and his demons are
real. They are part of the supernatural fabric of reality. This
being so, we begin to see that the reality of the presence of
the dragon in Tolkien's work is actually the very reverse of
its being a mere metaphor for man. It is not so much that
a fictional creature serves as an allegory of man but that a

real creature, the devil, is shown to us in a way that is easier
to see than is sometimes possible in our own cluttered and
myopic lives. In showing us the dragon which is wasting
fairyland, Tolkien is showing us the devil who is trying to
waste our own souls and those of all men. Seeing the dragon
as a mere metaphor is seeing it as a mirror which only
shows us the surface of human behavior; seeing the dragon
as representing the real presence of demonic evil in both
the story and the world beyond the story shows us a mirror
that does not merely reveal the surface of man's character
but the depths of his soul and the spiritual struggles being
waged there.

In practical terms, Tolkien's metaphysical understanding of reality means that the dragon sickness is not simply
about bad habits, such as acquisitiveness or possessiveness,
but about the sin that causes the bad habits, such as avarice and pride. Although this demonic dimension is present as potently in *The Lord of the Rings*, the dragon wears
more devious disguises in the latter work than he does in
The Hobbit. Take, for instance, Sauron, whose name resonates linguistically with *sauros*, the Greek word for lizard,
serpent or dragon, or Saruman, whose name is also suggestive anagrammatically of *sauros*. Closer to home linguistically is Wormtongue, whose name derives from *wyrm*,
the Old English word for dragon. Hence Wormtongue is
Dragontongue or Serpent-tongue. Tolkien plays with the
meaning of Wormtongue's name in Gandalf's commanding
rebuke, which reminds us of God's punishment of Satan in
the Garden of Eden: "Down, snake! Down on your belly!"
A few lines later, Gandalf emphasizes for a second time the

serpentine and demonic aspect of Wormtongue's character: "See, Théoden, here is a snake!" Finally, Wormtongue "bared his teeth; and then with a hissing breath he spat before the king's feet."[9] Wormtongue spits venom at the king as he had earlier spoken venom to him, poisoning him through the ear with his lies, much as King Claudius poisons Hamlet's father with physical poison in the ear and then poisons everyone else and the whole plot of the play with the poisonous lies that his lips convey to the poisoned ears of his dupes. And so we see that in *The Lord of the Rings* we are not presented with a dragon in its customary physical form, such as Smaug appears to us in *The Hobbit*, but we are presented instead with a variety of dragons in disguise, all of whom are afflicted with the self-same dragon sickness that pervades the earlier work. Sauron, a fallen angel, and Saruman, a fallen wizard, exhibit the dragon sickness in their obsessive desire to possess the Ring, whereas Wormtongue, a fallen Man, seeks to possess the king as a means of possessing the king's niece. In Sauron and Saruman the sin which causes the dragon sickness is pride, whereas in the pathetically shriveled and gollumized Wormtongue the cause of the dragon sickness is lust. In each case the characters are destroyed ultimately by their addiction to deadly sins.

We shall see presently how Smaug's own deadly addiction will lead to his own downfall. First, let's return to the narrative at the point in which Bilbo, protected by the ring and the cloak of invisibility which it provides, revisits Smaug on a reconnaissance mission and engages the dragon in a game of riddling which is reminiscent of the

episode under the other mountain with the miserable
Gollum. This time, however, it is not a riddling competi-
tion in which the participants take turns, but one in which
the hobbit teases the dragon in order to conceal his own
identity and to discover the dragon's weaknesses. Without
wishing to disclose his name to Smaug, Bilbo refers to himself in a series of ciphers. He is the "clue-finder," the "web-
cutter," the "stinging fly," and "he that walks unseen,"[10] all of
which is true but none of which is likely to present much
useful information to his adversary. Then he enunciates a
riddle, the meaning of which leaps from the page and from
the story itself with pyrotechnic brilliance as a revelation of
the book's deepest religious significance: "I am he that bur-
ies his friends alive and drowns them and draws them alive
again from the water."[11] On the literal level, this riddle refers
rather mundanely to Bilbo's "burying" of his friends in the
barrels in the elven-king's palace, "drowning" them when
the barrels are tossed into the river, and "drawing" them
alive again from the water when he releases them from the
barrels upon their arrival in Lake-town. On the allegorical
level, however, a Christian reader will hardly fail to see the
allusion to baptism. Our theological antennae attuned to
the clue being offered, we begin to see that the whole of
The Hobbit is a figurative account of Bilbo's baptism into
the fullness of life. He had been "dead" when trying to preserve the life of creature comforts at Bag End, his home in
the Shire, and needed to "die to himself," laying down his
life self-sacrificially for others, which is the hallmark and
meaning of love, in order to find the fullness of life. He had
to lose his life in order to gain it. He had to bury his old life

of self-centerdness in order to be resurrected into the new life of adventure. He had to risk death in order to find life. In short and in sum, he needed a baptism of death-defying and life-giving grace.

Considering the dragon's role in the story, it is no wonder that Smaug scoffs at this particular riddle, whereas he'd clearly been impressed by the earlier riddles and would find the riddles which follow it "better" than this less than "creditable" one. Smaug the Proud is suitably impressed by Bilbo's boasts that he is the "clue-finder," the "web-cutter," the "stinging fly," the "friend of bears," the "guest of eagles," the "Ring-winner," the "Luckwearer," and the "Barrel-rider," all of which are claims that might rightly be applied to a superhero who boasts of his strength, but the dragon scoffs at the riddle in which Bilbo's allusion to baptism comes closest to the words of Christ. Smaug has no interest in burying friends alive, drowning them, or bringing them back to life. He has no friends and devours his enemies with fire or eats them alive. For Smaug, the riddle of baptism is indeed not "creditable."

The clear allegorical aspect of the baptism riddle raises the question of the apparent introduction of Christ's voice into the narrative. Why are Bilbo's literal words possessed with the allegorical presence of the voice of Christ? The answer is best seen through a comparison with the demonic presence in *The Lord of the Rings*. We have seen how the demonic is disguised linguistically in the very names of Sauron, Saruman, and Wormtongue, suggestive of the presence of Satan in the characters themselves. Similarly, Bilbo's unwitting iteration of the words of Christ as the "I am" in the baptism riddle is suggestive of Christ's presence in and with Bilbo as he faces the dragon (Satan). Even though he doesn't know it, Bilbo is not alone as he faces his powerful Enemy (and let's not forget that *Satan* is the Hebrew word for *enemy*).

Ultimately the final confrontation between Bilbo and Smaug is a battle to the death between the humility of the hobbit and the pride of the dragon. As we shall see, and returning once again to the words of Christ, the proud will be humbled and the humble will be exalted.

CHAPTER 10

Dragon Pride
Precedeth a Fall

T HE BATTLE of wits between Smaug and the invisible hobbit culminates in Smaug's boast that he is indestructible and that he is far more powerful than any who are foolish enough to challenge him: "My armour is like tenfold shields, my teeth are swords, my claws spears, the shock of my tail a thunderbolt, my wings a hurricane, and my breath death!"[1]

Bilbo is understandably intimidated by such a brazen boast but asks whether it is true that dragons are more vulnerable underneath, especially in the region of the chest. Smaug retorts that Bilbo's information is "antiquated," and that he is covered with armor above and below. "No blade can pierce me," he gloats, and, as if to prove the point, and prompted by Bilbo's flattery about the dragon's fine waistcoat of diamonds, he rolls over to show the hobbit his dazzling armor. In doing so he inadvertently allows Bilbo to see that there is in fact an exposed patch of skin "as bare as a snail out of its shell"[2] on his left breast. Having discovered

Smaug's weak spot, Bilbo's reconnaissance mission is accomplished and he beats a hasty retreat up the tunnel from whence he came.

The positioning of the dragon's point of vulnerability directly over his heart (on the assumption that dragon physiognomy is the same as that of humans), conveys allegorical potency. Smaug's weak spot is not merely *over* the heart it is *of* the heart. It is the wickedness of his heart which will lead to his downfall. Recalling once again the words of Theoden and Gandalf that evil often hurts itself, we see that Smaug's pride has been his undoing. Having revealed his "Achilles' heel," we are reminded of other instances in literature of pride preceding a fall. We could begin indeed with Achilles himself, whose pride angers the gods and causes the deaths of countless Greek warriors including Achilles' closest friend. We recall Odysseus' boastfulness towards Polyphemos or the boastfulness of Penelope's suitors in Ithaka. Perhaps an even better parallel is the story of Chauntecleer from *The Nun's Priest's Tale* by Chaucer, in which Chauntecleer's downfall is caused by his boastful response to the fox's flattery. Chaucer's fable connects the pride of Chauntecleer allegorically to the Original Sin of Adam, thereby casting the fox in the role of Satan. Chauntecleer's subsequent fooling of the fox through the flattering of the fox's pride, turns the tables on the fox, signifying Chauntecleer's transformation into the New Adam (Christ). We can see that Tolkien's allegorical allusion to Christ in Bilbo's battle of wits with Smaug (Satan) resonates with Chaucer's approach, both writers thereby baptizing the age-old pagan moralizing about the destructiveness of pride or hubris with the presence of Christ's redemption of humanity.

Smaug, enraged by Bilbo's escape from his clutches and fearful that the "burglar" might return to steal more of his precious treasure, smashes the mountainside in the vicinity of the hidden entrance, trapping the hobbits and dwarves inside the tunnel with no apparent means of escape. The dwarves sink into despair but Bilbo "felt a strange lightening of the heart, as if a heavy weight had gone from under his waistcoat."[3] This "strange" feeling is similar to that experienced by Samwise Gamgee on the slopes of Mount Doom. After it becomes clear to Sam that Frodo lacks the necessary strength to climb the final stretch of the mountain, he resolves to try to carry Frodo himself, even though, in his own weakened state, he fully expects that he will not be able to do so. Sam staggers to his feet with Frodo clinging to his back, and "to his amazement he felt the burden light."[4] Christians reading this passage will be reminded instantly of the words of Christ that "my yoke is sweet and my burden is light" (Matthew 11:30). Considering that Sam is carrying Frodo, who, as the Ring-Bearer, i.e. Cross-Bearer, is a figure of Christ, this Gospel passage dovetails perfectly with Sam's situation: *Come to me, all you that labor and are burdened; and I will refresh you. Take up my yoke upon you and learn of me, because I am meek, and humble of heart; and you shall find rest to your souls. For my yoke is sweet and my burden light* (Matthew 11:28-30). Thus we are told that Sam might have received "some gift of final strength" and that he "lifted Frodo with no more difficulty than if he were carrying a hobbit-child pig-a-back in some romp on the lawns or hayfields of the Shire."[5] Clearly a Christian reader will see this "gift" as a miraculous fulfillment of the promise of the Gospel. It is a Divine intervention at the crucial moment as the Ring approaches its doom.

Compared with the doom-laden gravitas of Sam's amazement at his feeling his burden light, Bilbo's feeling of "a strange lightening of the heart" seems almost jovial, and yet it seems inescapable that the same "gift" has been given. On a deeper theological note, the varying response of the dwarves and the hobbit to the same "desperate" and "hopeless" situation is indicative of the state of their souls. Despair is a sin because it is the denial of the theological virtue of hope. It is inextricably connected to pride. The dwarves fall into despair because they have already fallen into pride. The hobbit, on the other hand, receives the gift of hope because he has humility. One is reminded of Chesterton's whimsically sagacious quip that "angels can fly because they take themselves lightly" whereas "the devil fell by the force of gravity," i.e. by taking himself too seriously![6] It is, therefore, not surprising that Bilbo, having received the "strange" gift of light-heartedness encourages his companions by reminding them that "while there's life there's hope."[7]

With the only safe escape route blocked, Bilbo and the dwarves have little option but to make their way towards the great hall in which the dragon had made his lair and in which all the treasure is hoarded. To their great relief they discover that the dragon is not at home, Smaug having flown off to attack Lake-town in his unquenched rage at the loss of the solitary trinket that Bilbo had taken from him. We should note, by the way, that Bilbo is not really a "burglar" or a thief. He is not stealing from the dragon because Smaug is himself the thief who has stolen the treasure from others. Bilbo had simply returned the treasure that he had "burgled" to Thorin, its rightful owner.

Discovering the unguarded treasure, the dwarves are ecstatic with excitement. Bilbo, however, is more level-headed and is not besotted by the mountain of wealth beneath his feet:

> Mr Baggins kept his head more clear of the bewitchment of the hoard than the dwarves did. Long before the dwarves were tired of examining the treasures, he became weary of it and sat down on the floor; and he began to wonder nervously what the end of it all would be. "I would give a good many of these precious goblets," he thought, "for a drink of something cheering out of one of Beorn's wooden bowls!"[8]

As with Bilbo's hopefulness when all the dwarves were desperate, he once again finds himself responding very differently from his companions to a common experience. Once again, the differing response is connected to the respective state of the hobbit's and dwarves' souls. The attachment and desire that the dwarves feel towards the treasure is a sign of the dragon sickness with which they are afflicted, an affliction that is described pointedly by the narrator as a "bewitchment." They are possessed by that which they would possess. Bilbo, on the other hand, sees more true wealth in the Franciscan simplicity of Beorn's hospitality, served up in humble wooden bowls, than all the opulence that the treasure hoard can offer. He is protected from the bewitchment of the dragon sickness by his humility, by his detachment and by his simplicity of heart.

Meanwhile, Smaug is wreaking havoc on the hapless and helpless people of Lake-town. Nothing can stop the dragon in his destructive rage, except the pride of the dragon himself. The old thrush, having heard of Smaug's prideful error in unwittingly showing Bilbo the unprotected weak spot on his left breast, conveys the news to Bard the Bowman. Bard only has one arrow left but he is helped by the providential rising of the moon at the exact moment that Smaug swoops in for the kill. The dragon's gem-encrusted body gleams in the moonlight, but not in the one place in which there are no gems and in which his body is exposed. Bard's arrow flies true to its mark and Smaug, with a deafening shriek, plunges to his death.

The way in which the dragon is killed is awash with Christian allegorical significance. He is killed by the darkness of his heart, symbolized by the absence of light reflected from the surface of the weak spot in his left breast. Delving even deeper into the theological applicability of the dragon's downfall we can see the connection between the light of the moon and the light of grace. We have seen how Tolkien uses the sun to signify the reflected light of God's presence, which disperses the shadow of evil. Here we see that the light of the moon, which is not really the moon's light at all but the reflected light of the sun, serves as a symbol of the grace of God. When the light falls onto the black hole of darkness or evil, no light of virtue is reflected.

The failure of the wickedness of the heart to respond to the light of grace is the cause of its spiritual death. Smaug's physical death is, therefore, a moral consequence of his spiritual death.

As with the setting of the sun which had providentially shown Bilbo and the dwarves the hidden door to Smaug's subterranean lair, the rising of the moon had providentially shown Bard the hidden door to Smaug's blackened heart. The courage of hobbits and men had been necessary for the defeat of the dragon, and so had the supernatural intervention of the hidden hand of Providence. We should not, however, forget the third crucial ingredient, as important and as indispensable to the dragon's defeat as human and hobbit virtue and providential aid. It was Smaug's own self-destructive pride which had been the ultimately necessary precedent for his fall.

CHAPTER 11

BILBO THE PEACEMAKER

THE DESTRUCTION of Smaug is in many ways the
climactic moment of the plot of *The Hobbit* in much
the same way as the destruction of the Ring is the climactic
moment in *The Lord of the Rings*. In both books, however,
the destruction of the Evil Thing, be it the dragon or the
Ring, does not destroy evil itself. In the latter book, the Shire
must still be scoured and Sharkey, the shriveled remnant
of Saruman, must be confronted. Similarly, in *The Hobbit*,
the death of the dragon does not lead to the healing of the
dragon sickness. On the contrary, the dragon's removal
seems to accentuate the evil effects of the sickness in the
dwarves, and in Thorin in particular. The portent of such
a problem is given by Tolkien in the very title of the chapter that follows the one in which Smaug is killed. Far from
peace and prosperity returning as we might have expected,
the chapter is called "The Gathering of the Clouds," signifying a coming storm. Furthermore, the allusive suggestion of
the "gathering of the clans," suggests that the storm that is
approaching is the storm of battle.

As news of Smaug's death spreads far and wide, thoughts of the legendary treasure under the mountain spread with it. Avaricious eyes turn towards the distant mountain and the now unguarded treasure that lies in wait for those who can claim it. Some have more claim than others. The people of Lake-town, whose homes were destroyed by Smaug in his anger at Bilbo's taking of the goblet, seek the treasure in compensation for their loss and to enable them to rebuild their town. The Elvenking amasses an army of spearmen and bowmen to march on the mountain, and the goblins, deep inside the Misty Mountains, are also eyeing the treasure with wanton desire. It is with this scenario in mind that Roäc the raven delivers news of Smaug's death to Bilbo and the dwarves, reminding Thorin that his small company of thirteen dwarves is a "small remnant of the great folk of Durin" who once lived under the mountain, and that therefore it would be wise to share the gold with men and elves so that peace might prevail.[1] It is implicit in Roäc's wise counsel that Thorin and the dwarves have no need for so much treasure and that thirteen dwarves and a hobbit cannot withstand the onslaught of the approaching armies of men and elves. Such wisdom is not heeded by Thorin who refuses to share the treasure, hoping that the dwarves of the nearby Iron Hills will come to his rescue. In the meantime, he resolves to prepare for a siege by fortifying the entrance to the cavern. Bilbo, who "would have given up most of his share of the profits for the peaceful winding up of these affairs," endeavors to remind Thorin that they have precious little food to withstand a siege but his warnings are ignored.[2]

As the dwarves are increasingly afflicted by the dragon sickness and the madness it causes, Bilbo finds himself isolated and alienated from his erstwhile friends and becomes increasingly uneasy at the turn of events. The arrival of the army of men and elves meets with defiance from Thorin whereas Bilbo longs to "join in the mirth and feasting by the fires" that he can see in the valley below. Even some of the younger dwarves mutter that "they wished things had fallen out otherwise and that they might welcome such folk as friends" but Thorin's angry scowl is enough to silence them.[3]

The injustice of Thorin's position is made manifest in Bard's efforts to reason with him. Bard announces himself as the one who has delivered the treasure into Thorin's hand by his slaying of the dragon. Does the slayer of the dragon have no claim on any of the gold? Bard also reminds Thorin that much of the treasure in the hoard was stolen by Smaug from the men of Dale after the dragon had destroyed their city. Does Thorin have the right to retain the gold of men, which had never belonged to the dwarves? Furthermore, Bard explains, Smaug had destroyed the dwellings of the men of Lake-town as a direct consequence of Thorin's arrival. Bard asks whether Thorin has "no thought for the sorrow and misery" of the people of Lake-town who had aided the dwarves in their distress.[4] Do the people of Lake-town deserve no recompense for the generous hospitality they had shown to the dwarves and for the destruction of their homes by the dragon, especially as Thorin's arrival had been the cause of the dragon's wrath?

The justice of Bard's words is unassailable. They are

"fair words and true," as the narrator tells us.[5] Hearing them, Bilbo feels sure that Thorin will heed the wisdom and common sense that they convey. The hobbit has not reckoned, however, with the power of the lust for gold in dwarvish hearts. "Long hours in the past days Thorin had spent in the treasury, and the lust of it was heavy on him."[6] Thorin defies Bard and refuses to negotiate with him. Bard, in turn, declares that Thorin and the dwarves are therefore placed under siege, condemning them to the fate and folly of Midas: "We will bear no weapons against you, but we leave you to your gold. You may eat that, if you will."[7] The final moral judgment on Thorin's disreputable action is given by Bilbo at the chapter's conclusion. "The whole place still stinks of dragon," he grumbles, "and it makes me sick."[8] His words serve as a double-entendre, working on two levels. On the literal level, he is referring to the stench of Smaug, which still lays heavy in the stale air of the cavern; on the deeper level, the "stink" is that of Thorin and his gold-lust, which is indistinguishable from the lust with which Smaug had guarded his hoard. Thorin, in his avarice and pride, has become the very dragon that he had sought to slay.

Some days later, Roäc brings news to Thorin that an army of dwarves from the Iron Hills is only two days' march away. In spite of bringing such "good" news, the raven is at pains to caution Thorin about the folly of his actions. The dwarvish army is only a little over five hundred in number and will probably not be a match for the besieging army of men and elves. Besides, Roäc adds, even were the dwarves to prove victorious, against the odds, their victory would still be a defeat. Winter and the snow, and the perils of the cold, will besiege them as surely as had the men and elves previously. "How shall you be fed without the friendship and goodwill of the lands about you? The treasure is likely to be your death, though the dragon is no more!"[9] The irony of Roäc's words is reminiscent of the words of Bard and Bilbo. Besieged by the elements, the dwarves will starve to death if all they have to eat is gold. Their "victory" will be as hollow as their stomachs, surviving the dragon only to be killed by the dragon's sickness.

Feeling that he must do something to broker peace between the two sides, Bilbo slips away from the besieged cavern, using the power of the ring, and delivers himself into the hands of the elvish guards. He is taken to Bard and the Elvenking, telling them in a repetition of the recurring reference to the morality of the Midas myth that Thorin "is quite ready to sit on a heap of gold and starve."[10] Bilbo then reveals the Arkenstone of Thrain, the brightest jewel in Smaug's ill-gotten treasury, which, as Bilbo explains, is "the Heart of the Mountain and . . . also the heart of Thorin [who] values it above a river of gold."[11] The priceless gem, which Bilbo had slipped into his pocket and kept secret from Thorin, will serve as a powerful bargaining tool. Bilbo's relinquishing of the Arkenstone, "not without a shudder, not without a glance of longing,"[12] is his own definitive recovery from the last vestiges of the dragon sickness from which he had himself been suffering, though in a much milder form than that which had afflicted Thorin. With impeccable moral sensibility, Bard asks Bilbo how the gem is his to give. Bilbo shifts uncomfortably and confesses that it isn't rightly his to give but adds that he is willing to let it stand in lieu of his rightful claim to one fourteenth of the treasure, as per his agreement with the dwarves.

Having given Bard and the Elvenking a weapon with which to broker peace, Bilbo shows yet another great feat of courage when he refuses the offer to remain in the safety of their camp, insisting instead on returning to the perils that await him with Thorin in the cavern under the mountain. As they pass through the camp, an old man, wrapped in a dark cloak, approaches them. "Well done! Mr Baggins!" he says, clapping Bilbo on the back. "There is always more about you than anyone expects!"[13] The mysterious stranger reveals himself as Gandalf, causing the hobbit's beleaguered heart to leap with delight. Whatever perils might await Bilbo when Thorin discovers that he has handed the Arkenstone to Bard seem relatively minor compared to the approval that he has received from the wizard. One imagines that such approval is worth more to Mr Baggins than countless Arkenstones.

On the following morning, Bard shows Thorin the Arkenstone and asks him if the return of the priceless gem might induce him to share some of the gold he is hoarding. Thorin is stunned into silence. When he speaks again it is with great wrath, accusing Bard and his allies of being thieves. "We are not thieves," Bard replies. "Your own we will give back in return for our own."[14] Thorin demands to know how Bard had received the Arkenstone, at which point Bilbo, quaking with fear, confesses that he had given it to him. In his rage, Thorin is on the verge of throwing Bilbo to his death on the rocks below and is only stopped by the timely interjection of Gandalf, who reveals himself and stays Thorin's hand. Bilbo justifies his actions by telling Thorin that he has disposed of his rightful share of the treasure as he wished. Having been dismissed contemptuously by Thorin, he joins Gandalf amongst the ranks of the men and elves.

As Dain and his small army of dwarves arrive to aid Thorin, it seems that a full-scale battle is inevitable. It is only averted by the arrival shortly afterwards of a huge army of goblins and wolves, forcing the dwarves, men, and elves into a hasty alliance against their common enemies. At the Battle of Five Armies, as it became known, the men of the Lake fight with long swords whereas the goblins wield scimitars. This places the battle symbolically as a clash between Christendom and the Infidel, the forces of goodness wielding the broad swords of the Christian crusaders whilst the forces of darkness fight with the curved swords of Islam. The same symbolism is employed in *The Lord of the Rings*, in which orcs are armed with scimitars whereas the men of Gondor fight with long swords. Equally significant in *The Lord of the Rings* are the characteristics of the exotic Southrons, men of the South, who serve the Dark Lord. The Southrons are also emblematic, in what might be called the "mind" of the West, of the ancient Islamic enemy. In this respect, Tolkien's approach owes much more to medieval works such as *The Song of Roland* than it does to modern literature.

After the battle, Bilbo is reconciled with the mortally wounded and contrite Thorin, who, healed of the dragon sickness, wishes to "part in friendship" and to apologize for his earlier words and deeds. Thorin tells Bilbo that he is going to the "halls of waiting" to sit beside his fathers "until the world is renewed."[15] Such words might seem superficially pagan or un-Christian but, on closer perusal, they can be seen to be entirely orthodox. Since the events in *The Hobbit* are taking place thousands of years before the Incarnation, the heroes of such an age do not have knowledge of the Heaven that is prepared for the virtuous by the Resurrected Christ. Christian orthodoxy asserts that the souls of those who died before the Death and Resurrection of Christ were in Limbo, a place of waiting, from which they were liberated by Christ Himself following His Resurrection, which is the moment when "the world is renewed." Christ's descent into "hell" following the Resurrection is depicted in many of the greatest works of art and is re-presented in thin disguise and with great subtlety in Aragorn's taking of the Paths of the Dead in *The Lord of the Rings*. Thorin's words are, therefore, profoundly orthodox from a Christian perspective, though of course he doesn't know it. This is but one instance of the extraordinary lengths to which Tolkien went in order to ensure that his own legendarium harmonized and dovetailed with orthodox Christian theology.

Bilbo's final words to Thorin are filled with a humble sorrow: "This is a bitter adventure, if it must end so; and not a mountain of gold can amend it. Yet I am glad that I have shared in your perils—that has been more than any Baggins deserves."

"No!" Thorin replies. "There is more in you of good than you know, child of the kindly West. Some courage and some wisdom, blended in measure. If more of us valued food and cheer and song above hoarded gold, it would be a merrier world."[16]

Much of the Christian morality of *The Hobbit* is conveyed in this final conciliatory exchange between Bilbo Baggins of the Shire and Thorin Oakenshield, the King under the Mountain. The adventure has been bitter, insofar as it ends in death, and no amount of material wealth can compensate for the loss of life. And yet Bilbo would rather have shared in the deadly perils of his friend, even in an adventure that ends so bitterly, than have stayed at home in the comfort of the Shire. In this embrace of suffering, even unto death, Bilbo is encapsulating the whole idea of life being a cross that we are called to carry willingly and indeed enthusiastically. Life is not about the pursuit of creature comforts and taking the paths of least resistance. It is about Love, which can be defined as willingly laying down our lives for others. In leaving the comfort of the Shire, our own "space" and comfort zone, and embracing the many crosses (sufferings) that the adventure (life) places in our path, and in giving ourselves willingly in the service of others, we grow in virtue, which is the only growth in stature that matters. Having experienced the adventure to the full, Bilbo is not only "glad" of all the pain and sorrow but feels himself unworthy to have been blessed with such suffering, which is "more than any Baggins deserves."

Faced at the point of death with such wisdom, it is no wonder that Thorin responds that there is more good in Bilbo, a "child of the kindly West," than the hobbit realizes.

He has courage and wisdom in right measure and values "food and cheer and song above hoarded gold." And here is the paradox at the heart of the Christian life: The one who embraces suffering, who dies to himself in order to die for others, is actually happier than the one who shuns suffering and who puts himself above all else. The most miserable people are those who are self-centerd, whose friendships are phoney, and who value material possessions over spiritual wealth. For in truth the Cross cannot be avoided. Everybody carries his cross and the one who resents it is nailed more painfully to it than the one who embraces it in an act of love. This is the secret of Christ's words that his yoke is easy and his burden light. If we allow Christ to help us carry our cross, we will find the very sufferings of life a source of joy; if we refuse His help we will be crushed under the weight of our sin's gravity.

After Thorin's death, Bilbo weeps until his eyes are red and his voice hoarse. In his sorrow he meditates on the apparent failure of his efforts to bring peace between Thorin and Bard:

> I wish Thorin were living, but I am glad that we parted in kindness. You are a fool, Bilbo Baggins, and you made a great mess of that business with the stone; and yet there was a battle, in spite of all your efforts to buy peace and quiet, but I suppose you can hardly be blamed for that.[17]

It is true that Bilbo's efforts to bring peace had failed. In the end, the dwarves, men, and elves could only be prevented from fighting each other by the timely arrival of the goblins and wolves. The forced alliance against a common enemy suggests that the hidden hand of Providence was the real peacemaker between dwarves, men, and elves, bringing them together in a common crusade against the forces of unequivocal evil. And yet Bilbo is right that he could "hardly be blamed" for the fighting, nor could he be blamed for the failure of his efforts to bring peace. Bilbo's actions were laudable and had faltered not because of any failure on Bilbo's part but because of the hardness of Thorin's heart. Ultimately his virtuous actions are a source of healing, prompting Thorin to apologize and to seek forgiveness. The reconciliation between dwarf and hobbit brings a peace between them, which, as Bilbo might say, is worth more than many mountains of gold.

As for Bilbo's self-confessed failure, we are reminded of the death of Boromir in *The Lord of the Rings*, which resembles the death of Thorin in its prevailing sense of contrition, penance, and reconciliation. "I have failed," says Boromir. "No!" replies Aragorn. "You have conquered. Few have gained such a victory. Be at peace!"[18] As a bringer of peace to the hardened heart of Thorin, Bilbo had not failed. He had conquered. He had gained a great victory. He was a consummate peace-maker and, as such, he could be at peace.

CHAPTER 12

BLESSED ARE THE POOR IN SPIRIT

AFTER THORIN is laid to rest, Dain becomes King under the Mountain and divides the treasure equitably. He desires to reward Bilbo "most richly of all."[1] The hobbit, however, declines his munificence. Assuring Dain that the treasure is better left in the dwarf's hands, and that, in any case, a simple hobbit would not know what to do with such a huge amount of wealth, he accepts only enough gold and silver that a strong pony could carry. "That will be quite as much as I can manage," he says.[2]

As Bilbo, accompanied on his long journey home by Gandalf, arrives at Rivendell he is once again greeted with elven song. This time the elves sing of mutability: of dragons that wither, their splendor humbled; of swords that rust, and thrones and crowns that perish; of the passing of the strength that men trusted and the wealth that they cherished. The transience of such things is contrasted with the enduring things of nature, such as grass, trees and rivers. The elves then sing of a theme that has woven its way through the length of the story:

The stars are far brighter
Than gems without measure,
The moon is far whiter
Than silver in treasure:
The fire is more shining
On hearth in the gloaming,
Than gold won by mining,
So why go a-roaming?[3]

Being open and alive to the gifts of Creation, such as moon and stars, and rivers, trees and flowers, protects us from the dragon sickness. Being blind to such gifts leaves us susceptible to the dragon's destructive power. Those who are open and alive, guided by the light of humility, will be blessed with the spiritual poverty with which they will inherit the kingdom of heaven; those who are blinded by the darkness of pride will be cursed with the material wealth with which they will purchase their ticket to hell. Such an understanding of reality, common to the elves of Rivendell and the Franciscans of Assisi, animates the whole moral atmosphere and literary dynamic of *The Hobbit*. Yet what do we make of the seemingly pointed question which the elven song asks? If it is true that the real treasures are the sun, moon and stars, and rivers and trees, all of which can be found fairly close to home, "why go a-roaming?" Was Bilbo's journey a waste of time? Should he simply have stayed at home?

As Bilbo's words to the dying Thorin made clear, he does not wish that he had stayed at home, nor does he think the journey a waste of time. On the contrary, he is grateful for the journey, in spite of its trials and tribulations, or perhaps because of them. If his goal in leaving home had been the attainment of "gems without measure," turning his back on his home and on the sun and stars in a lustful quest for gold, his journey would indeed have been one of folly. If his journey had been of this sort he would, no doubt, have succumbed to the dragon sickness of which the elven song seems to warn. The purpose of his journey, unknown to the reluctant hobbit upon his departure but no doubt part of Gandalf's purpose in inviting him to join the dwarves, was not material wealth but spiritual health. In short, the journey was a pilgrimage. This is made clear by Gandalf as he accompanies Bilbo home to the Shire. "My dear Bilbo!" the wizard exclaims. "Something is the matter with you! You are not the hobbit that you were."[4] The wizard in his wisdom perceives that the hobbit has grown. He had grown in moral stature; he had grown in wisdom; he had grown in virtue. In short, he had grown-up.

As Bilbo finally arrives home, more than a year after his departure, he is shocked to find that the contents of his home are being auctioned and that, indeed, most of his treasured belongings have already been sold for next to nothing. The auction was advertised as a sale of the property of "the late Bilbo Baggins Esquire" who was "Presumed Dead."[5] One can imagine the reaction as Bilbo gatecrashes his own vicarious funeral, so to speak, and declares in the words of Mark Twain that the reports of his death have been greatly exaggerated. We can imagine the shock but we might also be shocked to discover that the shock was an unpleasant one for some. The Sackville-Bagginses, Bilbo's nearest relatives, in anticipation of moving into Bag End and making it their own, were already measuring his rooms to see if their furniture would fit.

The legal ramifications of Bilbo's unexpected "resurrection" lasted for years. We are told that much time would elapse "before Mr Baggins was in fact admitted to be alive again."[6] Those who had got especially good bargains at the auction were not readily convinced that Bilbo's belated return necessarily meant that he was alive. In fact, to descend to the jargon of the lawyer, the fact that he was alive *de facto* did not equate with his being declared alive *de jure*. In the end, Bilbo was forced to buy back a good deal of his own furniture from those who were skeptical that he was legally "alive." His prized silver spoons disappeared without trace, presumably at the avaricious hands of his nearest relatives. As for the Sackville-Bagginses themselves, "they never admitted that the returned Baggins was genuine, and they were not on friendly terms with Bilbo ever after."[7] Having coveted his home, they never forgave him for returning to it.

In one important respect, Bilbo's closest relatives were closer to "home" than might be imagined, in the sense that the Sackville-Bagginses could be seen as a mirror of what Bilbo might have become if he hadn't embarked on his pilgrimage. Their unhealthy attachment to "home" and its accoutrements and their lack of detachment had turned them into petty Smaugs, defined by the dragon sickness with which they are afflicted. In this context, it is surely significant that Bilbo doesn't learn until the very end of the story of the tragic fate of the Master of Lake-town, another petty Smaug, who, like the Sackville-Bagginses, is also pathetically shriveled and gollumized by the dragon sickness. We are told that the Master had come to "a bad end": "Bard had given him much gold for the help of the Lake-people, but being of the kind that easily catches such disease he fell under the dragon-sickness, and took most of the gold and fled with it, and died of starvation in the Waste, deserted by his companions."[8] Deserted in the desert, he dies of the gold-induced hunger which could have been the fate of Thorin had the hand of Providence not intervened to rescue him from himself.

Bilbo's return to the Shire after his adventurous wanderings also mirrors the return home of the hobbits in *The Lord of the Rings*. In both works, the protagonists do not return to the halcyon home of a remembered arcadia but to a home beset with microcosmic manifestations of the evils that had beset them in their adventures. In the later work, the inheritance of the Shire, as a whole, is being sold-off by those who had caught the dragon sickness, much as Bilbo's own inheritance is being sold-off in *The Hobbit*. Returning to the tuneful musings of the elves on the subject of mutability, we are being reminded of the entropic consequences of the Fall, which means that everything is subject to the decay caused by sin. There is no going back to a "pure" past, which was, in any case, not really pure; we can only work tirelessly in the present to preserve and restore the inheritance of the past from the ravages of time. As Chesterton reminds us, if we leave a thing alone we do not leave it as it is, we leave it to a "torrent of change," most of which will be for the worse. To employ Chesterton's metaphor, if we want to preserve a gatepost, we do not leave it alone; if it is to be preserved we have to continually be painting it.[9] Thus the Shire must be scoured upon the hobbits' return in *The Lord of the Rings* and Bilbo must fight for his very "life," so to speak, upon his return home and must work hard to restore Bag End to what it had been upon his departure.

As with the first person "I am" in Bilbo's riddling with Smaug, we cannot see the "death" and "resurrection" of Bilbo at the story's end purely at face value, which is to say we cannot see it solely on the literal level of meaning. Bilbo is "presumed dead" and yet remarkably rises from his presumed death in the very midst of his *de facto* "funeral." Such "death" and "resurrection" seems to demand an allegorical connection to scripture. Returning to Gandalf's words shortly before Bilbo arrives home, we can see that Bilbo is not the hobbit that he was. He had been spiritually "dead" before he set out on his adventure, much as the Sackville-Bagginses are "dead" upon his return. His journey had changed him. It had brought him to life. It was the death of the old Hobbit and the birth of the new. He had been "born again." It was a baptism into a truer, fuller life. In this sense the perception of his resurrection from the dead upon his return is only a literal recognition of a deeper spiritual reality. Bilbo had indeed been dead but is now alive.

The fact that Bilbo's "resurrection" is not accepted by those who are spiritually "dead," such as the Sackville-Bagginses and their ilk, who know the price of everything and the value of nothing, reminds us of those who refused to accept the Resurrection of Christ after He rose from the dead and of the words of scripture in which Christ prophesied this rejection of His Life: *If they hear not Moses and the prophets, neither will they believe, if one rise again from the dead* (Luke 16:31). Thus Bilbo, in spite of the new life that is in him, is considered dead in the eyes of the world. We are told that he has lost much more than his spoons—"he had lost his reputation . . . he was no longer quite respectable."[10] The loss of such worldly reputation and worldly respectability means very little to the "resurrected" Bilbo. He no longer cares for such trifles. If he is dead in the eyes of the world, he is also dead to the world. He no longer seeks the things that the world has to offer, having discovered the pearl of great price that the world does not value.

The stealing of the treasure from Bilbo's own kingdom—and let's not forget that a hobbit's home is his castle—reminds us of Bilbo's own role as a "burglar" who "stole" the treasure from the dragon. It is, however, an inversion of Bilbo's role and not a parallel with it because Bilbo was not really a burglar or a thief. He was merely taking from the dragon that which the dragon had stolen from others. Furthermore he did not take the treasure for himself but to return it to its rightful owner. The parallel scenario, as distinct from its inversion, would be to see the Sackville-Bagginses and the other pillagers of Bilbo's possessions as images of Smaug, invading the kingdom of another, despoiling it, and seeking to claim it as their own. Another parallel scenario is to see Bilbo's return as a reflection of the return of the king. Like Thorin and Aragorn, though on a much smaller scale as is appropriate for a hobbit, Bilbo returns to his kingdom to claim his true inheritance. If

Thorin is the King under the Mountain, Bilbo is the king under the hill, his home address being "Bag End, Underhill, Hobbiton." His kingdom might be miniscule in relation to Thorin's or Aragorn's but, for a hobbit, that which is small is all the more beautiful for its smallness. Like Thorin, he faces his own dragons and frees his hobbit-hole kingdom of their presence. His return is truly the return of the king and, in the light of his "resurrection," we can see the aptness of the phrase that is uttered upon the death of one monarch and the accession of his successor: *The King is Dead, Long Live the King.* The old king of Bag End is indeed "dead," long live the new king.

The new king of Bag End rules his kingdom in a radically different way from the old king. Whereas the old Bilbo was very protective of his reputation and desired to be seen as "respectable" by his neighbors, we are told that the new Bilbo "did not mind" the loss of his reputation and respectability: "He was quite content: and the sound of the kettle on his hearth was ever after more musical than it had been even in the quiet days before the Unexpected Party."[11]

Home is sweeter for the absence. Everything is made new, even the smallest things, *especially* the smallest things, such as the kettle on the hearth. The new Bilbo sees the old things with new eyes and he sees that they are good, indeed better than he had ever imagined them to be.

In the final conversation between Gandalf and Bilbo, with which the story concludes, Gandalf reminds the hobbit that he is but a small part of a much bigger providential picture:

You don't really suppose, do you, that all your adventures
and escapes were managed by mere luck, just for your
sole benefit? You are a very fine person, Mr Baggins, and
I am very fond of you; but you are only quite a little fellow in a wide world after all!"

"Thank goodness!" said Bilbo, laughing, and handed
him the tobacco-jar.[12]

The final paradox, worthy of Chesterton or indeed of
Jesus Christ, the latter of whom is the Master of paradox
as he is the Master of everything else, is that the purpose of
Bilbo's pilgrimage was to enable him to grow big enough to
know how small he is. The greatest gift that Bilbo receives
from all his adventures is the poverty of spirit which
enables him to inherit the kingdom of the heaven-haven of
the Home. And since every true home is but an image and
prefigurement of the ultimate Heaven-Haven for which we
are all made, Bilbo's kingdom is closer than he realizes to
the Kingdom of God.

When Gandalf proclaims that Bilbo is no longer the
hobbit that he was, we know that he is changed for the
better. He no longer places his heart at the service of his
worldly possessions but seeks instead those treasures of the
heart to be found in wisdom and virtue. He is healed and he
is whole, or, as Tolkien the Catholic might say, he is whole
because he is holy. The hobbit has attained the habit of virtue and, as befits the hero of any good fairy story, he knows
what is necessary to live happily ever after.

TOLKIEN AND THE
TRUTH OF FAIRY TALES

Ever since I arrived at Cambridge as a student in 1964
and encountered a tribe of full-grown women wearing puffed sleeves, clutching teddies and babbling
excitedly about the doings of hobbits, it has been my
nightmare that Tolkien would turn out to be the most
influential writer of the twentieth century. The bad
dream has materialized. At the head of the list, in pride
of place as the book of the century, stands *The Lord of
the Rings*.[1]

THESE DISMAL words expressing disgust that *The
Lord of the Rings* had been voted the greatest book of
the twentieth century in a major national opinion poll in
the UK were written by the militant feminist, Germaine
Greer, who rose to fame in 1970 as the author of *The Female
Eunuch*, one of the most influential books of the women's
liberation movement. Why, one wonders, does Tolkien's

magnum opus have the power to give his critics nightmares? What is it about Tolkien's work that causes such an
apoplectic reaction? The answer was provided by Greer
herself in her complaint that Tolkien's work was an escapist
"flight from reality":

> Most novels are set in a recognizable place at a recogniz-
> able time; Tolkien invents the era, the place, and a race
> of fictitious beings to inhabit it. The books that come in
> Tolkien's train are more or less what you would expect;
> flight from reality is their dominating characteristic.[2]

Greer's criticism of *The Lord of the Rings*, which is of
course equally applicable to *The Hobbit*, is common to most
of Tolkien's detractors. Such critics, who pride themselves
on what they perceive as their "realism", see Tolkien's work
as the stuff of mere fantasy, a childish escape into the realm
of the fairy story. The best response to these attacks was
supplied by Tolkien himself with erudite eloquence in his
definitive essay "On Fairy Stories"[3] in which he confronts
the implicit assumption inherent in the modern materialist *weltanschauung*, or worldview, that fairy tales are unreal,
and therefore irrelevant and impertinent.

According to Tolkien, fairy tales assist in the "recovery" of the human spirit: "Recovery (which includes return
and renewal of health) is a re-gaining . . . of a clear view,"
and entails "seeing things as we are (or were) meant to see
them." Fairy tales access a reality beyond the mundane
world of *facts*, enabling *meaning* to permeate the factual.
Such stories go beyond seeing things only as they are, or
as they seem to be; they see them as they are meant to be.

They do not accept the status quo, merely because it is the 'real world', but explore the possibilities of different and better worlds. They transcend the barren limitations of 'how things are' to explore the fruitful possibilities of 'how things should be'. This intrinsic idealism clearly has implications as regards the way that fairy stories interact with reality. They challenge our blindness to the beauty and inherent meaning of the world around us.

Tolkien's discussion of "Escape and Consolation", two other beneficial facets of fairy stories "which are naturally closely connected", focuses on a defense of "escapism" against "the tone of scorn and pity with which 'Escape' is now so often used: a tone for which the uses of the word outside literary criticism give no warrant at all." Detecting the ideological animus behind the critical animosity to "escape," Tolkien accused his accusers of seeking to imprison the imagination within the stifling walls of materialistic presumption. "Why should a man be scorned if, finding himself in prison, he tries to get out and go home? Or if, when he cannot do so, he thinks and talks about other topics than jailers and prison-walls? The world outside has not become less real because the prisoner cannot see it." Tolkien then implies that the materialistic critics are themselves the jailers, treating "the Escape of the Prisoner" as "the Flight of the Deserter": "Just so a Party-spokesman might have labeled departure from the misery of the Führer's or any other Reich and even criticism of it as treachery." The real reason, therefore, behind the prejudice against, and the hostility towards, fairy tales on the part of many literary critics is purely a prejudice against, and a hostility towards, metaphysics in general, and Christianity in particular.

Among the reasons why we desire escape, Tolkien ranks "oldest and deepest" the "Great Escape: the Escape from Death." And even though fairy stories might provide many examples of an escape from mortality into immortality, Tolkien states clearly that these are stories "made by men and not fairies." We can hear strong echoes of his own mythology in his next remark that the "Human-stories of the elves are doubtless full of Escape from Deathlessness." Immortality for those, such as the elves, who are blessed or cursed with it, is truly a great burden, an "endless serial living," and, Tolkien insists, the fairy tale is "specially apt to teach such things." Immortality is to be trapped in time and unable to escape from its interminable confines. For the immortals, therefore, death might seem a means of escape into another and better place. In thus illustrating the difference between time and eternity, the fairy story can open reality to new and exciting metaphysical vistas.

The ultimate Consolation of fairy stories is the "joy of the happy ending." Tolkien says that this joy is neither "escapist" nor "fugitive" as a critic might term it. On the contrary, it is "a sudden and miraculous grace." Tolkien reveals his Christian theology as he describes the "piercing glimpse of joy, and heart's desire, that for a moment passes outside . . . the very web of the story, and lets a gleam come through." This radiance is nothing less than the hope that all Christians bear for the final "happy ending." This is the most powerful consolation offered by fairy stories: "All tales may come true; and yet, at the last, redeemed, they may be as like and as unlike the forms that we give them as Man, finally redeemed, will be like and unlike the fallen that we know."

APPENDIX B

WISDOM IN WONDERLAND

As a means of illustrating Tolkien's understanding of the truth to be found in fairy stories, this short essay contrasts the view of Tolkien, and others such as G. K. Chesterton and C. S. Lewis, with that of the worldly cynic and the materialist critic.

"ONCE UPON a time," said kind Uncle Chestnut, "we were all little children and we lived in a place called wonderland." Looking up from the book of fairytales that he was reading for the umpteenth time, he smiled sadly at his nephew. "The problem is that we forget that we were children and we lose sight of wonderland . . ."

"Enough!" exclaimed his nephew, who had recently completed his first semester at college. "Enough of such saccharine sentimentality! Enough of this Never-Never Land naiveté! That stuff is for innocent kids, uncle. You're old enough to know better. Isn't it time you grew up?"

Uncle Chestnut put the book to one side. "Innocent?

Grown up? None of us were ever truly innocent and some of us never grow up."

"Well," said the nephew, whose name was Eustace, "I wish *you* would grow up!"

So, who is right? Uncle Chestnut? Or Eustace? Is wonderland merely a place for wishful thinking? Is it just for children?

"When I was a child," says St. Paul, "I spoke as a child, I understood as a child, I thought as a child: but when I became a man, I put away childish things." Isn't St. Paul agreeing with Eustace? Shouldn't Uncle Chestnut put away childish things and just grow up? But what of the words of Christ: "Unless you be converted and become as little children, you shall not enter into the kingdom of heaven." Clearly St. Paul would not disagree with these words of his Mentor, his Master; clearly, therefore, St. Paul means something different when he speaks of those things that are childish from what Christ means when He speaks of the necessity of becoming child-like. It is this paradoxical difference between childishness and childlikeness that holds the key to understanding the difference between the relative perspectives of Uncle Chestnut and Eustace.

The first thing we need to remember is that Christ Himself is a storyteller. He teaches many of His most important lessons through the telling of stories, or parables to give them their "grown-up" name. We think of the Prodigal Son perhaps, or the Good Samaritan, two fictional characters who, as figments of Our Lord's imagination, become figures of truth for all generations. He tells us stories because we are His children and these stories are the best way for us to understand what He means to tell us. If we will not become child-like, listening like children, we will not see the truth in the story, the moral that it teaches. The fact that the Prodigal Son or the Good Samaritan never existed in the "real world" but only as characters in the story does not make them less real. On the contrary, they become such powerful archetypes that there have been countless "prodigal sons" or "good Samaritans" in every generation since Christ first told the story.

And what is true of these stories can be true of other stories, each of which is the product of the God-given gift of the imagination. This is what Uncle Chestnut means when he praises wonderland and laments that we forget the wonderland we experienced as children. It is not that we forget that we were children, it is that we forget that we are children. There are some, to be sure, the victims of wicked stepmothers (or stepfathers), whose experience in wonderland was not much fun. There are others, led astray by ugly sisters or uglier friends, who turn their wonderland into a place of real ugliness. We forget, at our peril, that wonderland is not only full of wonders but wicked witches also. We forget that wonderland does not only contain wolves but, much more dangerous, wolves in sheep's (or grandma's) clothing. Wonderland is not a place of idyllic and unrealistic innocence or naiveté, as Eustace seems to believe, but a place where the virtuous struggle heroically against wickedness. In short, it is very much like the world in which we actually live.

But wait a minute, we can hear Eustace exclaim, the world in which we actually live does not have wolves that disguise themselves as granny. It does not have magic wardrobes through which we can pass into other worlds. It does not have beautiful princesses that sleep for a hundred years until a noble prince awakens them with a kiss. It does not have pumpkins that turn into carriages. At this point, Uncle Chestnut might remind his nephew that the world is full of wolves who disguise themselves as sheep or grannies. They include baby-kissing politicians, or advertising executives who launch marketing campaigns employing traditional values to sell poisonous products. He might also remind Eustace that every good book or good movie is a magic wardrobe that transports us to other worlds. Perhaps he might smilingly suggest that his nephew is himself a sleeping beauty who needs to be awakened by the kiss of goodness and truth. And as for pumpkins, Uncle Chestnut would insist that a pumpkin is more miraculous than a carriage and that we should learn to be as astonished at the appearance of the pumpkin on our plate as was Cinderella with the appearance of the carriage on the night of the ball.

On a more wistful note, the kindly uncle might warn his nephew that there are real dangers in not believing in the real magic of wonderland. There is a real danger that those who do not believe in dragons become dragons. There is a real danger that those who do not believe that Jack could slay the Giant become servants of the Giant and slayers of Jack. Such people, who are very successful in politics and law, are placed in the Giant's pocket and are used

by him to ensure that Jack remains powerless and that the
Giant's monopoly over the goose that lays the golden egg
is safeguarded.

The cause of the singular blindness that prevents people
from seeing the wisdom of wonderland is that people know
their abc's but have forgotten their p's and q's, their *please*
and *thank yous*. To say "please" is to ask for something in
the proper manner, to say "thank you" is to show the appropriate gratitude. This is true of our relationship with our
friends and family but is especially so of our relationship
with God. It is no surprise that *please* is connected etymo-
logically with *plea* and *plead* and is, therefore, connected
practically to the reality of prayer. More important, the act
of thanksgiving is a sign of our gratitude for the wonders
of Creation and for the wonders of our existence within it.
Giving thanks, showing gratitude, is a sign of humility and
it is to the humble of heart that the vision of wonder is given.
An ungrateful heart that believes it has nothing for which
to be thankful is a proud heart incapable of wonder. As if
by magic, wonderland becomes invisible to these proud-
hearted souls. They cannot see it and therefore believe that
it does not exist. This is, of course, the warped and defective
logic of the relativist. For this sort of "realist" all reality is
in the eye of the beholder. As such, all reality that they do
not behold is ipso facto unreal: *"I do not see it, therefore it is
not real."* Needless to say, such logic is childish and here we
return to the difference between the childish and the child-
like. The childish, lacking gratitude, fall into the sin of cyni-
cism that blinds them to the beauty of truth; the childlike,
grateful for the gift of life, see through the eyes of wonder

and behold the wonderful wisdom of wonderland. And this beautiful vision is but a shadow of the Beatific Vision, the ultimate Wonderland where people truly live happily ever after.

NOTES

Chapter 1

1. Humphrey Carpenter, ed., *The Letters of J. R. R. Tolkien* (New York: Houghton Mifflin, 2000), p. 172

2. J. R. R. Tolkien, *The Monsters and the Critics and Other Essays* (London: George Allen & Unwin, 1984), p. 125

3. Colin Manlove, *Modern Fantasy: Five Studies* (Cambridge: Cambridge University Press, 1978), pp. 182-83

4. J. R. R. Tolkien, *The Lord of the Rings* (London: Harper Collins, 2004), p. 585

5. Ibid., p. 595

6. G. K. Chesterton, *The New Jerusalem* (London: Thomas Nelson and Sons, 1920), p. 159

Chapter 2

1. J. R. R. Tolkien, *The Hobbit* (London: Harper Collins, 1988), p. 13

2. James Hardy, ed., *The Denham Tracts, Volume 2*, London: Folklore Society, 1895

3. Tolkien, *The Hobbit*, p. 13

4. Ibid., p. 14

5. Ibid., pp. 15-16

6. Ibid., p. 17

7. Ibid., p. 16

8. Ibid., p. 32

9. Ibid., p. 33

Chapter 3

1. Hilaire Belloc, *The Four Men* (London: Thomas Nelson & Sons, 1948 edn.), p. 35

2. Ibid., p. 38

3. Although it is fairly safe to assume that Tolkien was familiar with the tale of St. Dunstan, as told by Belloc, it should be conceded that Tolkien was also very widely read in English folklore, and especially in the folklore related to Saxon England prior to the Norman Conquest. As such, it is likely that he had read several versions of this story and would have known that the legend that Belloc ascribes to St. Dunstan is more often ascribed to St. Cuthman.

4. See Martin C. D'Arcy, *Laughter and the Love of Friends: Reminiscences of the Distinguished English Priest and Philosopher* (Westminster, Maryland: Christian Classics, 1991), pp. 112-113.

5. Tolkien, *The Hobbit*, p. 55

6. Tolkien, *The Lord of the Rings*, p. 56

7. Tolkien, *The Hobbit*, p. 60

8. Ibid.

Chapter 4

1. Tolkien, *The Hobbit*, p. 69

2. Humphrey Carpenter, *J. R. R. Tolkien: A Biography* (London: George Allen & Unwin, 1977), p. 91

3. Carpenter, ed., *The Letters of J. R. R. Tolkien*, p. 53

4. Ibid., p. 111

5. Tolkien, *The Lord of the Rings*, p. 1

Chapter 5

1. Tolkien, *The Hobbit*, p. 74

2. Ibid.

3. Ibid., p. 75

4. Ibid.

5. Ibid., p. 77

6. Ibid., pp. 81-82

7. Ibid., p. 82

8. Michael Alexander (translator), *The Earliest English Poems* (Harmondsworth: Penguin Classics, 1966), p. 71

9. Tolkien, *The Lord of the Rings*, p. 357

10. Tolkien, *Letters*, p. 255

11. Tolkien, *The Hobbit*, p. 83

12. Tolkien, *The Hobbit*, p. 85

13. Ibid.

14. Ibid., p. 87

15. Tolkien, *The Silmarillion* (New York: Ballantine Books, 2002), p. 6

16. Tolkien, *The Hobbit*, p. 90

17. Tolkien, *The Lord of the Rings*, p. 59

18. Ibid., p. 59

19. Tolkien, *The Hobbit*, p. 90

20. Ibid., p. 92

Chapter 6

1. Tolkien, *The Hobbit*, p. 96

2. Ibid.

3. Ibid., p. 97

4. Ibid., p. 114

5. Ibid., p. 120

6. Tolkien, *The Lord of the Rings*, p. 258

7. See Michael D. C. Drout, ed., *J. R. R. Tolkien Encyclopedia* (New York: Routledge, 2007), p. 56

8. Tolkien, *The Hobbit*, p. 126

9. Ibid., pp. 134-5

10. Ibid., p. 135

11. Ibid., pp. 136-37

12. Ibid., p. 137

13. Ibid., p. 148

14. Ibid., p. 152

15. Ibid.

16. Ibid., p. 170

17. Ibid.

18. *Daily Telegraph*, 21 January 1997

Chapter 7

1. Tolkien, *The Hobbit*, p. 174

2. Ibid., p. 184

3. Ibid.

4. Ibid. p. 188

5. Ibid., p. 190

6. Carpenter, ed., *The Letters of J. R. R. Tolkien*, p. 255

7. Tolkien, *The Lord of the Rings*, p. 862

8. Tolkien, *The Hobbit*, pp. 192-93

Chapter 8

1. Tolkien, *The Hobbit*, p. 190

2. Ibid., p. 193

3. Ibid., p. 201

4. Ibid., p. 60

5. Ibid., p. 202

6. Ibid.

7. Tolkien, *The Lord of the Rings*, p. 702

8. Ibid.

9. Ibid., p. 909

10. Roy Campbell, *Selected Poems*, London: Saint Austin Press, 2001, p. 46

11. Charles Causley, *Collected Poems, 1951-2000*, London: Picador, 2000, p. 352

12. Tolkien, *Letters*, p. 255

13. J. R. R. Tolkien (ed. Christopher Tolkien), *The Monsters and the Critics and Other Essays*, London: George Allen & Unwin, 1984, pp. 156-7, emphasis added.

Chapter 9

1. Tolkien, *The Hobbit*, 203

2. Ibid.

3. Ibid., p. 204

4. Ibid.

5. Ibid., p. 206

6. Ibid.

7. Ibid., p. 207

8. Ibid., p. 208

9. Tolkien, *The Lord of the Rings*, p. 520

10. Tolkien, *The Hobbit*, p. 212

11. Ibid., p. 212

Chapter 10

1. Tolkien, *The Hobbit*, p. 215

2. Ibid., p. 216

3. Ibid., p. 222

4. Tolkien, *The Lord of the Rings*, p. 941

5. Ibid.

6. G. K. Chesterton, *Orthodoxy*, London: John Lane, The Bodley Head, 1921, pp. 221-222

7. Tolkien, *The Hobbit*, p. 222

8. Ibid., p. 227

Chapter 11

1. Tolkien, *The Hobbit*, p. 244

2. Ibid., p. 245

3.   Ibid., p. 247

4.   Ibid., p. 249

5.   Ibid.

6.   Ibid.

7.   Ibid., 250

8.   Ibid.

9.   Ibid., p. 252

10.   Ibid., p. 255

11.   Ibid., p. 256

12.   Ibid.

13.   Ibid., p. 257

14.   Ibid., p. 259

15.   Ibid., p. 270

16.   Ibid., pp. 270-71

17.   Ibid., p. 271

18.   Tolkien, *The Lord of the Rings*, p. 414

Chapter 12

1.   Tolkien, *The Hobbit*, p. 273

2.   Ibid., p. 274

3.   Ibid., pp. 277-78

4. Ibid., p. 281

5. Ibid., p. 282

6. Ibid.

7. Ibid.

8. Ibid., pp. 284-5

9. Chesterton, *Orthodoxy*, pp. 210-11 "... *all conserva-tism is based upon the idea that if you leave things alone you leave them as they are. But you do not. If you leave a thing alone you leave it to a torrent of change. If you leave a white post alone it will soon be a black post. If you particularly want it to be white you must be always painting it again ...*"

10. Tolkien, *The Hobbit*, p. 282

11. Ibid., pp. 283-4

12. Ibid., p. 285

Appendix A

1. *W Magazine*, Winter/Spring 1997; quoted in Joseph Pearce, *Tolkien: Man & Myth*, San Francisco: Ignatius Press, 1998, p. 6

2. Ibid.

3. J. R. R. Tolkien, *The Monsters and the Critics and Other Essays*, pp. 109-61. All quotes are taken from this essay.

About the Author

THE AUTHOR of more than fifteen books, Joseph Pearce is the foremost Catholic biographer of the past two decades. He has chronicled the life and works of, among others, J.R.R. Tolkien, C.S. Lewis, and William Shakespeare. Pearce is also the co-editor of *The Austin Review*, Executive Director of Catholic Courses, and host of the EWTN program, *The Quest for Shakespeare*. He is Writer in Residence and Visiting Fellow at Thomas More College of Liberal Arts in Merrmack, New Hampshire. He is also Visiting Scholar at Mt. Royal Academy in Sunapee, New Hampshire.

The Hidden Meaning of *The Lord of the Rings*

The Theological Vision in Tolkien's Fiction

Joseph Pearce

Despite the absence of any direct mention of Christ or the Catholic Church, Tolkien described The Lord of the Rings *as "fundamentally religious and Catholic." He endowed his protagonists with Christian virtues, and incorporated themes of grace and mercy.*

Course No. C500

Professor Joseph Pearce

Over the eight lectures in the course, Professor Pearce highlights connections, allegories, and insights which will expand your reading of *The Lord of the Rings*. It is said that art holds the mirror up to life. This is the reason that art is "real" and fiction is "true". *The Lord of the Rings* enjoys such fame and popularity because in a way, it shows us ourselves in the characters. Learn more and discover for yourself the truth written into *The Lord of the Rings* with Professor Joseph Pearce.